祝
ワンダリングドッグ
結成!!
ROSE GUNS DAYS
Season2
2

Contents

Rose Guns Days
Season 2

A FEW MONTHS BACK

UGH...
DOKA (POW)
GA (THUD)

〈FUCKING JAPANESE...〉
〈YOU CAN'T DO THAT TO MY PEOPLE!!〉
〈DIE!〉
HYU (FWISH)

SU (FWOOSH)
!

GOKI (CRACK)
GWAHH!
DOSA (THUD)
UGH...
DAMN CHINESE. GANGING UP ON ME...

Track 06: Good Time

KARAN (CLATTER)

OLIVER! WHERE'VE YOU BEEN?

SETTLING A MATTER WITH SOME CHINESE BASTARDS.

GA (GRAB)

WAYNE-SAN TOLD US TO TAKE CARE OF IT TOGETHER...!

IS THAT BLOOD...? HOW'D YOU "SETTLE" IT!?

THEY WEREN'T THE TALKING TYPE...
...SO I CRUSHED EVERY LAST ONE INTO THE DIRT.
...WE WERE SUPPOSED TO SOLVE THE ISSUE PEACEFULLY!
THAT WAS WAYNE-SAN'S ORDER!

BAN
(SLAM)
!
ZA
(STEP)
YOU
REALLY...
...TOOK CARE
OF SOME OF
OUR YOUNG
FELLOWS,
IT SEEMS.
SHIT!
THAT'S THE
GOLDEN
DRAGONS'—
...
HMPH.
PRETTY
CHILDISH,
COMING
WITH A MOB
TO BACK
YOU UP.
BUT OF
COURSE...
YOU'RE THE
ONE WHO
TURNED
THIS INTO
A PLAY-
GROUND
FIGHT...
...
AREN'T
YOU?

SEEING AS THAT'S THE CASE...
......
ZA
...WE'VE COME WITHOUT ANY "ADULT" WEAPONS.
BULLETS WOULD BE WASTED...
...TORMENTING A MEWLING WHELP LIKE YOU.
TREATING ME LIKE A KID...?
HOW DARE YOU—
SHU (F-WOOSH)
!
FU (SHIFT)

TON (WHAP)
...!?
GAHH!
DOSA (THUD)
WE CHINESE LOOK OUT FOR OUR OWN.
HEH.
SO EVERYTHING YOU DID TO OUR BOYS...
HEH.
...IS ABOUT TO COME BACK TO YOU.
HEH HEH HEH ...

AND THEN ...
...WHAT HAPPENED?

HE GOT THE TAR KICKED OUTTA HIM.
ONLY REASON 'E LIVED IS 'COS IT'D BE BAD FER BUSINESS T'KILL 'IM...

IT EVEN WENT PAST WAYNE-SAN, ALL THE WAY UP T'CYRUS-SAN, 'N THE END. REAL BIG DEAL...
CAUSED A MESS OF TROUBLE FER EVERYONE.

THAT'S ...
... NO GOOD.

IF YOU'RE GONNA LAUGH, JUST DO IT...

!
...I'M NOT LAUGHING.
...YOU SHOULD BE.

I'D FEEL BETTER ABOUT IT IF YOU DID.

OH?
FINE, THEN.
KARA (CACKLE)
UGH ...

GU (YANK)
...COME ON.

SHA (FWIP)

DO YOU WANNA FEEL SORRY FOR YOURSELF? I DON'T THINK SO.

WHAT YOU WANNA DO IS RESTORE YOUR REPUTATION AND GET WAYNE-SAN TO RECOGNIZE YOU. RIGHT!?

MY REPUTATION'S ALREADY ...

WAYNE-SAN THINKS I'M NOTHING...

ZUI (THRUST)

IF WAYNE-SA REALLY HATED YOU...

...HE'D HAVE BOOTED YOU OUTTA THE WILD DOGS A LONG TIME AGO!

!

BUT HE DIDN DO THA DID HE
THAT'S PROOF HE STILL SEES YOU AS A COMRADE!

WAY—
...WAYNE-SAN... THINKS... THAT?

...WE'RE GONNA RESTORE THAT HONOR OF YOURS.

I GUARANTEE IT!

—...
....
OLI-VER?
YOU'RE...

...TOO CLOSE!
BE-SIDES, YOU GUYS ...
...YOU HAVE SOME PRETTY NCRED-IBLE ALENTS, HUH?

IT'S LIKE YO SAID A THE BA EARLIE NINA.
YOU JUST DIDN'T HAVE YOUR INSTRUMENTS ON HAND.
YEAH, 'BOUT THAT...

THE GEEZER WHO USED TO RUN THIS SHOP TAUGHT US HOW TO PLAY.
HE KICKED THE BUCKET NOT TOO LONG AGO, THOUGH.

HE LET US LIVE HERE IF WE AGREED TO TAKE HIS MUSI LESSONS
WEIRD OLD GUY, REALLY.
HE SAID THAT KIDS LEARNING MUSIC...
...WAS IMPORTANT TO KEEP THE LIGHT ALIVE, IN THESE TIMES.

HE WAS STRIC AS HEL ACTU-ALLY.
REALLY?

I WANNA HEAR THIS. COME ON. PLAY SOME-THING.
......

I'M JUST NOT INTERESTED IN THAT ANYMORE...

..DON'T EXPECT MUCH OUT OF ME.
GATA (CLATTER)
ガタ
GATA
ガタ

POOON (DING)
ポーン
POOON
ポーン
HAVEN'T TOUCHED THIS THING IN AGES.
RIGHT, RIGHT.
Y'CAN SAY THAT AGAIN!
WE'RE NO PRO ORCHESTRA, YA HEAR?

JUST A TROUPE OF STREET RATS.
YEAH... THIS IS ONLY BECAUSE YOU ASKED, ZEL.
GATA
ガタッ

SO LIKE IT OR NOT, HERE WE GO.

I CAN'T WAIT!

PHONE CALL FOR YOU FROM LITTLE ZEL.
!

FROM ZEL?

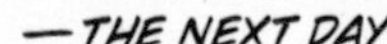
—THE NEXT DAY

DON
(BOOM)
BAR PARCHITA 23
ZEL...
WE REALLY GONNA BE ALLOWED TO PERFORM HERE?
YUP!

SURE THIS'S THE RIGHT PLACE...?
SO BIG.
IT IS, I SWEAR!
AND YOU REALLY GOT MADAM ROSE'S PERMISSION FOR THIS?

YES, OF COURSE!
AFTER ALL, IT WAS MERYL-SAN WHO GOT US CONNECTED TO THIS CLUB.

STEP LIVELY NOW!
LET'S GET YOU INTRODUCED TO THE OWNER.
GUI
GUI (SHOVE)

WE'VE BEEN EXPECTIN YOU YOUNGSTERS!
NO WAY I COULD TURN DOWN AN INTRODUCTION FROM MERYL-SAN!!
THANKS FOR HAVING US.
WE'VE GOT THIS OLD SECOND-HAND UPRIGHT, BUT...
...THERE'S NEVER BEEN ANYONE TO PLAY IT.

SO PLAY TO YOUR HEART'S CONTENT!!
BAN (BAM)

YOU ARE. I PROMISE.

EEP...
YOU KNOW WE'VE NEVER ACTUALLY PLAYED FOR A LIVE AUDIENCE, RIGHT?
HISO
HARD TO IMAGINE WE'RE GOOD ENOUGH FOR A PLACE LIKE THIS...
HISO (WHISPER)

YOU'RE NOT THE DUNCES THEY MADE YOU OUT TO BE.
SO LET'S PROVE IT!

BAR PAR

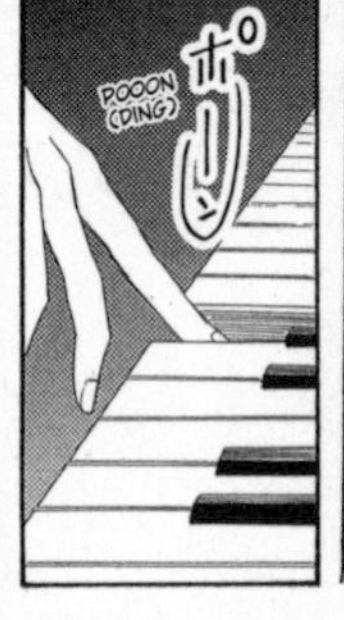
POOON (DING)

POOON
THAT'S A RARE THING.
THEY ROM A IEARBY SCHOOL OR SOME-THING?

AH HA HA HA...
HYU (SIGH)

AH...
THOSE EYES...

FILTHY.

...LIKE THEY'RE STARING AT A COUPLE OF CORPSES ...

HURRY UP AND DIE, YOU LITTLE RATS.
I SHOULD'VE BEEN PISSED, BUT...

...JUST LIKE MY STOMACH, MY HEAD WAS TOTALLY EMPTY.
COULDN'T FEEL A DAMN THING EITHER WAY, BACK THEN.

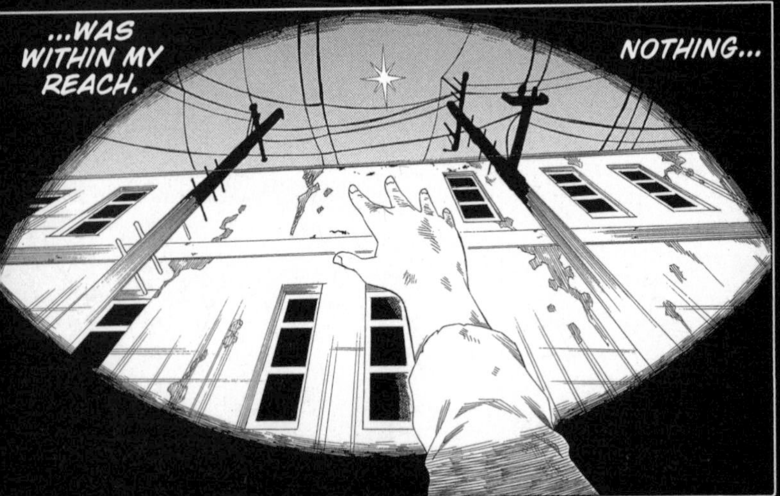
NOTHING...
...WAS WITHIN MY REACH.

PASHI (GRAB)
!
COME WITH ME.
MUSIC IS NEEDED IN THIS WORLD, AND SO ARE YOU.

FOR US, WITH NOTHING ELSE...
ACCEPTING THAT KINDNESS ...

LEARNING FROM HIM...

...EVEN LOSING HIM...WAS SIMPLE...

HUH?

...THE OLD MAN.

JYAN (TADAA)

YEAHHHH!

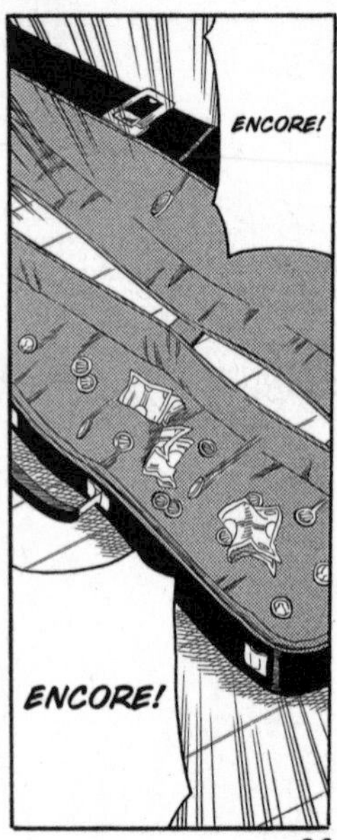
ENCORE!
ENCORE!

ENCORE!
EH-HEH-HEH ...
OLD MAN...
GATA (STAND)

PACHI (CLAP)

PACHI

THE OLD MAN WAS JUST...!

TCH...

PACHI (CLAP)
PACHI
BRAVO!!

...ZEL.
SEE!? JUST LIKE I TOLD YOU, OLIVER!

YOU'RE NOT DUNCES AT ALL!

ZEL...
......

!
PASHI (GRAB)

GUI
(TUG)
OLIVER!?

...SING.

EH...

EHH!!?
C'MON,
SING
FOR US!

BUT I... ALL I'VE EVER DONE IS A LITTLE HUMMING!
PASHI (FLING)
THE TUNE YOU'RE ALWAYS HUMMING, THEN.

...CAN'T RUN AWAY AFTER COMING THIS FAR, ZEL.

WE'RE NO TRIO.

WE'RE A QUARTET.

POOON (DING)

POOON
ポーン

POOON
ポーン

POOON
ポーン

...THAT WAS HOW...

...WE BECAME MORE THAN ROOM-MATES.

WE WERE A QUARTET. EVERYONE SHARING FROM THE POT.

AND WHEN WORD OF US SPREAD THROUGHOUT TOWN...
...THEY DIDN'T HAVE ANY CHOICE BUT TO SEE US.

TO RECOGNIZE...
...THAT WE WEREN'T JUST A BUNCH OF DUNCES.
19:00 ~ 20:30
LIVE in the

OOH!

WHO KNEW ZEL WOULD HAVE A TALENT FOR SINGING?

THEY'RE GETTING A PRETTY GOOD REP, SO THEY'RE MAKING THE ROUNDS AT MY CLUBS.

I HEAR THAT THEIR LIVE PERFORMANCES HAVE DONE WONDERS TO PREVENT DRUNKEN BRAWLS.

PERHAPS MUSIC REALLY DOES HAVE THE POWER..
...TO BRING PEACE TO THIS WORLD OF OURS.

—...

WAYNE.
!

DO YOU HAVE A MOMENT?
...SURE.

ABOUT THE PLACEMENT OFFICE MATTER...
...I HEAR RUMORS THAT THE GOLDEN DRAGONS ARE MANEUVERING IN SECRET.
...RUMORS, HUH? ANYTHING SPECIFIC...?
I'M NOT SURE.

THE INFORMATION CAN'T BE VERIFIED, SO I HAVEN'T BROUGHT THE NEWS TO ROSE YET.
BYUUU (WHOOSH)
...STILL...
...THESE ARE THE GOLDEN DRAGONS WE'RE TALKING ABOUT.

IT'S ENTIRELY POSSIBLE THAT THEY SHAKE HANDS WITH THEIR RIGHT WHILE CONCEALING A DAGGER IN THEIR LEFT.

......

......
GOT IT.
I'LL LOOK INTO IT.

ZA (STEP)

WHAT-EVER IT IS...

IN THIS WORLD WE LIVE IN, YOU'RE BOUND TO FIND SOMETHING BY OVERTURNING SOME STONES.

WE NEED A TRUMP CARD TO MAKE THE GOLDEN DRAGONS REVEAL THEIR HAND.
ROSE ...

Track 07: Axel F

BAR
Bar

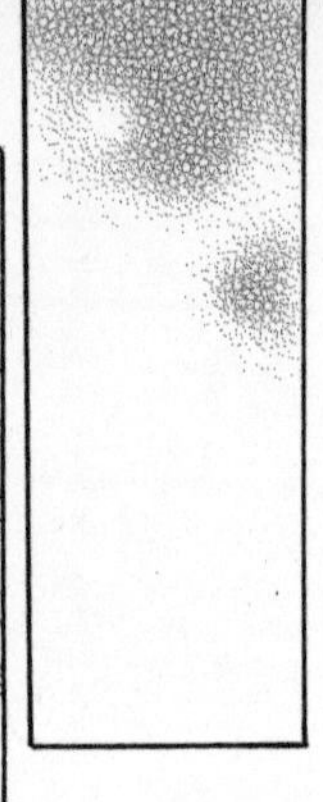

THIS IS ON THE HOUSE!
THANKS FOR THAT PERFORMANCE!
WOOOW!

Let's dig in!!

NEVER THOUGHT WE COULD ACTUALLY MAKE IT AS MUSICIANS.
AND I'M MORE SUITED T'THIS THAN LISTENIN' T'CUSTOMERS DRONE ON.

...NOT BAD, I GUESS.

...SO YOU STILL...
...WANT TO LIVE AS ONE OF THE WILD DOGS?

...WHILE CRAWLING ON MY BELLY IN THE GUTTER BACK THEN...
...I ALWAYS WANTED TO BE A GUY WHO COULD WALK WITH A SWAGGER IN HIS STEP.

BUT GETTING STANDING OVATIONS, AND GETTING PAID FOR IT...
...ISN'T THAT BAD, I GUESS...
ONE TIME.

JUST A SINGLE, SOLITARY TIME.

WELL DONE, OLIVER.
I WANTED TO HEAR HIM SAY THAT TO ME.

...TIME TO WAKE UP FROM THAT DREAM THOUGH. THE WRITING'S ON THE WALL.
LOOKS LIKE WE FINALLY FOUND OUR CALLING, HUH?

......
GATA (STAND)
SORRY FOR KILLING THE MOOD!

!
PASHI (GRAB)
IT'S FINE, OLIVER!

...
NO MATTER HOW TALENTED YOU ALL ARE WITH THE MUSIC...
...I KNOW YOU'VE STILL GOT THE SPIRIT OF THE WOLF IN YOU.
YOU'RE WILD DOGS AT HEART.
AND I KNOW THAT!

Y'SEE, I...
I KNOW THAT... AND I GOT YOU STARTED WITH ALL THESE PERFORMANCES FOR A REASON...
...WITH A GOAL IN MIND...!

A GOAL ...?

... WELL ...
CHIRA (GLANCE)

THINK ABOUT THE KIND OF CUSTOMERS WE'RE SEEING AT ALL THESE BARS AND CLUBS...
HISO (WHISPER)
WHAT KIND DO WE SEE A LOT OF?

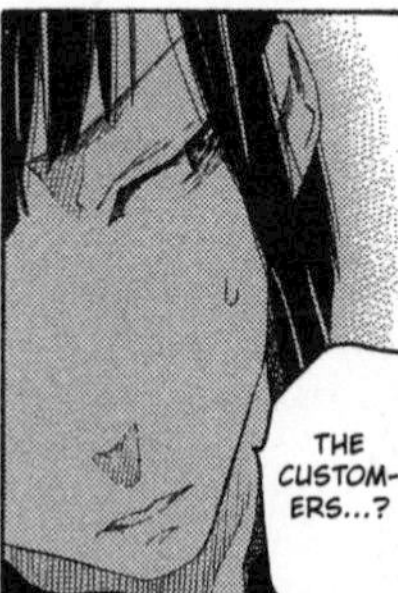
THE CUSTOM-ERS...?

THEY'RE ALL GRUMBLING ABOUT NOT FINDING WORK...

NOTHING BUT DAY LABORERS, LOOKS LIKE.

!

NO WAY...

?
STILL GOT NO CLUE WHAT YOU'RE TRYING TO TELL US...
ZEL...
DID YOU REALLY...?

YES.
WE'RE HERE TO GATHER INFORMATION!

WAYNE-SAN NEEDS TO KNOW ABOUT THE TROUBLE OUT IN FRONT OF THE PLACEMENT OFFICE.
SO I THOUGHT WE MIGHT BE ABLE TO HELP HIM OUT!

THE "BACKDOOR OFFICE" ...

KOTSU (SKRITCH)
BACKDOOR OFFICE
THAT'S THE KEY PHRASE I'VE BEEN HEARING FROM CHINESE LABORERS AT ALL THESE JOINTS.

SO LISTEN.
THIS IS WHAT THE JAPANESE WORKERS HAVE BEEN COMPLAINING ABOUT.

PAPERS: BIG SALE, BARGAIN BLOWOUT

WAGES MIGHT'VE GONE UP, BUT THESE OUTSIDERS ARE KEEPING US FROM GETTING ANY JOBS...
AT THIS POINT WE'RE LUCKY TO WORK ONCE IN TWO DAYS...

SO WAGES HAVE GONE UP...
...WHICH LURES IN MORE OUTSIDERS.
THEN IT SEEMS LIKE THERE'S LESS WORK OVERALL...

MOST PEOPLE THINK THAT, SO THEY JUST HAVEN'T NOTICED...
CKDOOR OFFICE
Take us!!
We've got work for you.
OUTSIDERS
PEOPLE OF DISTRICT 23
...BUT SOME HAVE DEFINITELY PICKED UP ON THE FACT...

...THAT THE TRUCKS THEMSELVES ...
We've got work for you.
...AREN'T SHOWING UP ANYMORE.

HEY...WE'RE NOT SEEING MANY TRUCKS LOOKING FOR WORKERS, RIGHT?
REALLY? CAN'T BE SURE. JUST TOO MANY PEOPLE OUT FOR JOBS FOR US TO GET ANY.
NAH! THERE'RE SOME EMPLOYERS WHO JUST HAVEN'T SHOWN UP LATELY.

SFX: GARI (SCRATCH)

?
SO WHERE'RE THESE TRUCKS DISAPPEARING TO?
I GET IIIT...

THEY'RE OVER AT THIS "BACKDOOR PLACEMENT OFFICE"!

HUH?
HOW DENSE ARE YOU...? LISTEN.

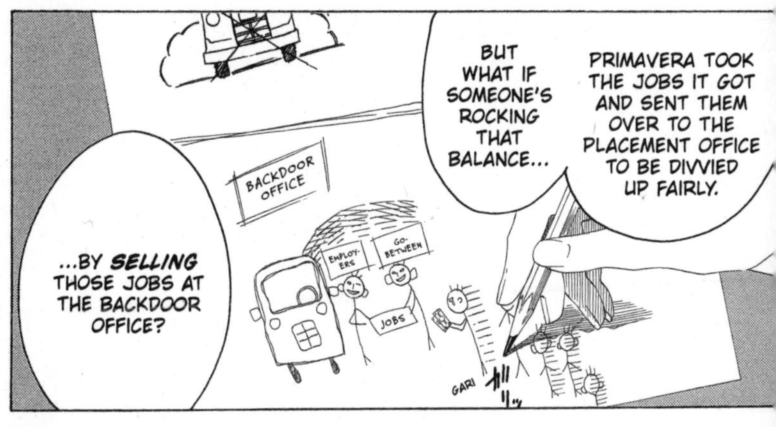
PRIMAVERA TOOK THE JOBS IT GOT AND SENT THEM OVER TO THE PLACEMENT OFFICE TO BE DIVVIED UP FAIRLY.
BUT WHAT IF SOMEONE'S ROCKING THAT BALANCE...
...BY *SELLING* THOSE JOBS AT THE BACKDOOR OFFICE?
BACKDOOR OFFICE
EMPLOY-ERS
GO-BETWEEN
JOBS
GARI

HEY.
SHUT YOUR TRAP.
BESHI (WHAP)
USED TO BE THAT ONE DAY OF LABOR EARNED A MAN TWO HUNDRED DOLLARS.
BUT THANKS TO MADAM ROSE, THAT DOUBLED TO FOUR HUNDRED DOLLARS.
NOWADAYS, THOUGH, IF A GUY CAN ONLY FIND WORK ONCE EVERY OTHER DAY...
...THEN HE'S RIGHT BACK DOWN TO AN AVERAGE OF TWO HUNDRED DOLLARS PER DAY.

SO THEN, IF SOME BASTARD SHOWS UP OFFERING THE JOBS FOR $210 EVERY DAY...
...THE WORKERS ARE GONNA JUMP AT THAT CHANCE WHETHER THEY LIKE IT OR NOT.

GATA (STAND)
RIGHT!
SO THE GO-BETWEENS LINE THEIR POCKETS WITH THE OTHER $190!!

THE GUYS LIVIN' FAT 'N' HAPPY FROM THESE KICK-BACKS...
...MUST BE THE ONES DOIN' BUSINESS AT THIS "BACKDOOR OFFICE" SCAM!!
YES.

FINDING OUT THE REAL STORY BEHIND ALL THIS IS OUR JOB, AS WILD DOGS.
BACKDOOR OFFICE
IF WE CAN NAIL DOWN PROOF OF WHAT'S GOING ON...
...THAT'LL BE A PRETTY FEATHER IN OUR CAP, RIGHT!?

ALL RIGHT... TOMORROW, WE HEAD TO THE PLACEMENT OFFICE!
GATA (STAND)
BEING ON THE SCENE MIGHT LEAD US TO SOME CLUES.

YOU'RE THERE FOR INFORMATION ONLY.
SO YOU HAVE TO AVOID MAKING A SCENE!

PROMISE ME, OLIVER?

...SURE.

—IN FRONT OF THE PLACEMENT OFFICE

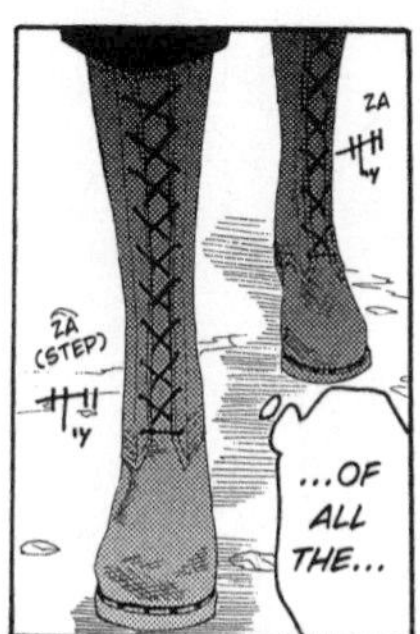
ZA
ZA (STEP)
...OF ALL THE...

WHY'D I HAVE TO DRESS LIKE THIS...?
I LOOK LIKE AN OVER-GROWN STREET RAT!
ZA
ZA

ONE HOUR EAR-LIER

YOU'LL BLEND RIGHT IN AND BE ABLE TO TALK TO PEOPLE THIS WAY!

I CALL IT, "PLACEMENT OFFICE LABORER FASHION"!

PLUS, YOU LOOK REALLY SHARP!

HERE.

......

CHIRA (GLANCE)

......

KYU (WEAK)
SHARP... EH?
MPH.

SHIT...
I HEAR PRIMAVERA'S GONNA CHASE AWAY THESE OUTSIDERS SOONER OR LATER...
HERE'S HOPING SOONER.
...OH.

NOW'S MY CHANCE!!
AHEM...
...TOO BAD WE HAVEN'T SEEN ANY TRUCKS LATELY.

HUH?
LESS JOBS... IT SEEMS.
I HEAR YA.
DEFINITELY LESS WORK THESE DAYS.
I HEAR THERE'S SOMEWHERE ELSE AROUND HERE A GUY CAN GO TO FIND A JOB.

WHERE'
THAT!?
I WOULDN'T BE TWIDDLING MY THUMBS HERE IF I KNEW.

BUT...
...THERE'S A GENTLEMEN'S AGREEMENT IN PLACE THAT SAYS WE LABORERS CAN ONLY BE RECRUITED HERE AT THE PLACEMENT OFFICE.
YEAH, BUT IT'S NOT LIKE WE CAN EXPECT THE EMPLOYERS TO REALLY HONOR THAT.
...NOW THAT YOU MENTION IT...

THERE'S ONE TRUCK THAT DEFINITELY HASN'T COME AROUND RECENTLY.
YOU KNOW THE ONE.
THAT OLD CUE-BALL RECRUITING MEN TO HAUL CARGO DOWN AT THE PORT...

THE OLD MAN WITH THE BUMP ON HIS NOGGIN? IT'S TRUE. HAVEN'T SEEN HIM AROUND HERE.
BUT I SAW HIM YESTERDAY AT THE PORT.
THROWING HIS WEIGHT AROUND, SAME AS EVER.
...THIS BALD GUY...

WAHHH!
FOUR HUNDRED DOLLARS FOR A DAY'S WORK!
NEED TEN GUYS TO CLEAN THE SEWERS!

WAHHH!
!

WHERE COULD HE BE HIRING, THEN...?

DON (THUD)
TCH ...

STOP RIGHT THERE!
GUWA (ROAR)
!

NO ONE'S INTERESTED IN CHATTING NOW...
ZARI (SKRITCH)
BETTER HEAD HOME AND REPORT TO ZEL...

YEH JUST STEPPED ON MY FOOT!

SO HAND OVER YOUR WALLET, NICE AND EASY!

...

SHUT YOUR TRAP, SCUM.
WHAT'S ONE THING GOT TO DO WITH THE OTHER?
I'M TALKIN' ABOUT COMPENSATION FOR MY INJURY. 'COS I CAN'T WORK NOW.
KI (GLARE)
GOT IT? SO MAKE IT QUICK...

PIKU (TWITCH)

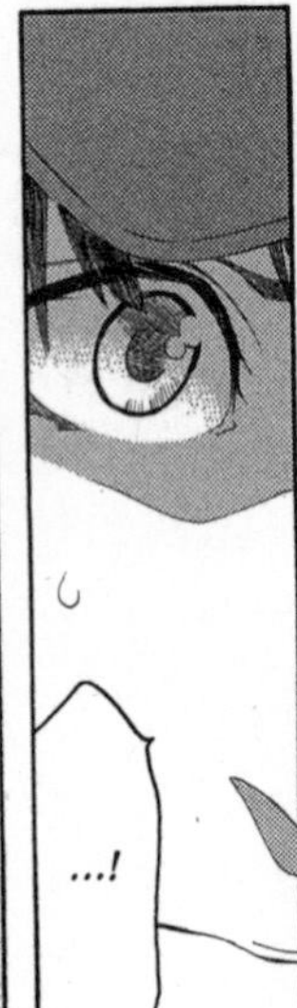
...!

PROMISE ME?

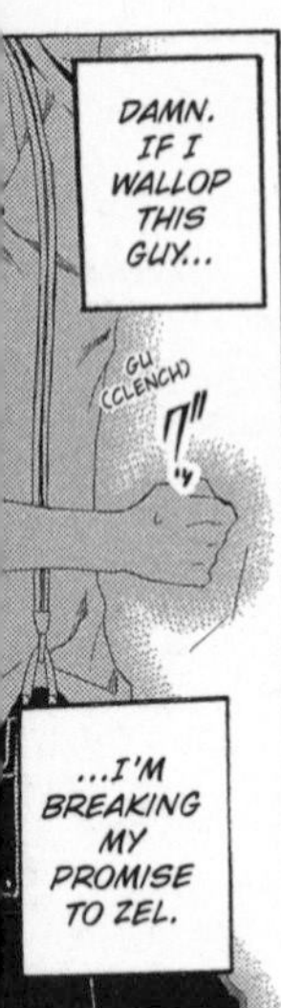
DAMN. IF I WALLOP THIS GUY...
GU (CLENCH)
...I'M BREAKING MY PROMISE TO ZEL.

YOU EVEN LISTENIN', KID!?

DOSU (POW)

GU
...
GAKU (SLUMP)

GET UP!
DOGO (WHAM)

SHIT...THIS BASTARD'S RUNNING THE OLDEST SCAM IN THE BOOK.
...
DOSA (THUD)
AND I CAN'T EVEN TALK BACK!?

ME? I CAN'T FIGHT BACK...!?
SAY SOME-THING!
GA (WHAP)
OUCH.

GA (GRAB)
YOU JUST PUNCHED ME IN THE HEAD!
WHAT IF THAT PUT ME IN THE HOSPITAL? HOW WOULD YOU PAY FOR THAT?
WHAT!?
WHAT'RE YOU ACCUSING ME OF!?
...!
HEY, GET BACK HERE.
DA (DASH)
HAA.
HAA.

HAA! HAA!
...

THAT HURT ...

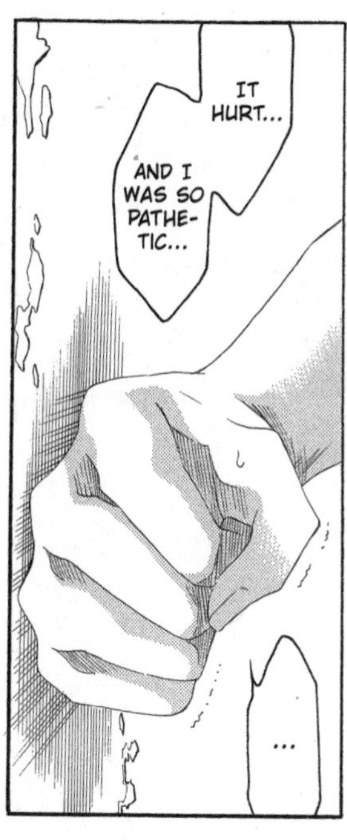
IT HURT...
AND I WAS SO PATHETIC...
...

RUNNING FROM A FIGHT'S THE MOST PATHETIC THING THERE IS!!

GOD-DAMMIT!

HAA. HAA.

PFFT...

WONDER WHAT THEY'LL HAVE TO SAY...
...WHEN I TELL THEM I RAN AWAY FROM A FIGHT...
TA (TMP)

WHAT THE?
OLIVER GOT HURT? OUR OLIVER?

I WAS SURE YOU'D JUST COME HOME FROM ANOTHER FIGHT.
HE'S UNFAZED !!

CHARLES. STOP EATIN IT ALL YERSELF 'N' HELP SET THE TABLE!
AWW, MAN.
CHARLES AND NINA JUST CAME BACK FROM CHECKING OUT THE PORT.
YEP.

WE WERE SURE TO MAKE OURSELVES NICE AND DISGUISED!
WELL, NINA?
UGH... SO TIGHT... 'ROUND MY CHEST...
NOT THAT!

LOOKING AT THIS SCENE, ARE WE REALLY SUPPOSED TO BELIEVE THERE'S LESS WORK AROUND?
WAA (YAP)
WAA
HARD T'SWALLOW, YEAH. S'LIKE THE PAPERS SAID...
THE CARGO FROM AMERICA FER POST-WAR RECOVERY OR WHATE'ER'S COMIN' IN STRONG.
THEY NEED ALL THE SPARE 'ANDS THEY CAN GET...!

YA HEAR ME!?
!

NOT A ONE OF YOU'S IRREPLACEABLE.
GASHI (KICK)
GASHI
GUH ...
GUYS'RE LINING UP TO TAKE YER SPOT!!

IF YOU WANT THAT DOUGH, EAT DIRT AND WORK YOUR ASSES OFF!
GAH-HA-HA-HA-HA-HA!

... HUH?
...!
WHAT'RE YOU BRATS LOOKING AT?

JUST SHOWING UP HERE'S NOT GONNA GET YOU A JOB.
GO AND LINE UP OUTSIDE THE PLACEMENT OFFICE LIKE EVERYONE ELSE.
...
KUI (PRESS)
... WELL ...

NOT THAT I'D PAY A PENNY TO HIRE A GANGLY LITTLE THING LIKE YOU.
GAH-HA-HA-HA-HA-HA!
GIRIRI (CLENCH)
THAT BALD BASTARD ...

MAKES ME SICK JUST T'REMEMBER 'IS STUPID FACE!!
PAKOOON (WHACK)
OUCH!
HEY!

DON'T WORRY. WE GOT A LITTLE PIECE OF PAYBACK.
GOSO (RUSTLE)

WHILE EVERYONE WAS LOOKING THE OTHER WAY...

TA-DAAA! GOT THIS FROM HIS WALLET.
DOOON (BAM)
AN ID CARD WITH A SNAPSHOT OF HIS MUG!!

AND WHAT IF YOU'D CAUSED A SCENE, PULLING THAT OFF!?
I RETURNED HIS WALLET WHERE IT CAME FROM. I SWEAR.
... THIS GUY.
THAT'S NOT THE ISSUE HERE...

THE OLD MAN WITH THE BUMP ON HIS NOGGIN?

THIS COULD BE THE BASTARD THOSE GUYS WERE TALKING ABOUT...
GOSHI (RUB)

OWWWWWWW!!
IF SO, IT'S LIKELY THAT HE'S HIRING WORKERS FROM SOMEWHERE ELSE...
SURE IS
ISPICIOUS.
GOSHI
GOSHI

BOTTLE: DISINFECTANT

I'M REALLY SURPRISED YOU DIDN'T FIGHT BACK THOUGH, OLIVER!
THAT'S A GOOD BOY.

ONLY 'COS YOU SAID...!
?

ONLY BECAUSE YOU MADE ME PROMISE...
WH— ...

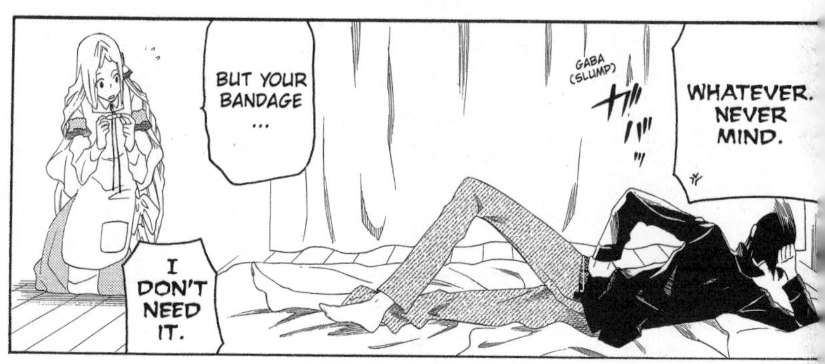
WHATEVER. NEVER MIND.
GABA (SLUMP)
BUT YOUR BANDAGE ...
I DON'T NEED IT.

Y'SURE ARE HANDY T'KEEP AROUND, ZEL.
WHO THE 'ELL WERE YOU A'FORE Y'LOST THOSE MEMORIES?
AH HA HA...
THINKING ABOUT THAT'S...
...KINDA SCARY.

IF ZEL'S MEMORIES COME BACK ALL OF A SUDDEN...
...WHO KNOWS WHERE SHE'LL RUN OFF TO...?

......
...S'GOT NOTHING TO DO WITH HER PAST.

ZEL IS JUST ZEL.
IF HER MEMORIES COME BACK...

...AND WE LEARN SHE NEEDS HELP WITH SOME-THING...
...WE'LL BE THERE.
SO...

DON'T JUST UP AND VANISH ON US.
BASA (FWIP)
......

...UM-
HUM.

THANK YOU, OLIVER.

CHINA-TOWN
GAYA (CHATTER)
GAYA

<SO...YOU'RE SAYING WE'RE GUARANTEED JOBS?>
<SO IT'S LIKE A BACKDOOR TO GET WORK, HUH...?>
<THE KICKBACKS THEY'RE TAKING ARE ROUGH, BUT...>
<...S'BETTER THAN WAITING AROUND UNTIL KINGDOM COME AT THE PLACEMENT OFFICE.>
......

<S'WHY THEY CALL IT THE "BACKDOOR OFFICE"...>
BINGO!

THAT'S THE ONLY WORD I NEEDED TO HEAR.
GATA (STAND)
NOW I JUST GOTTA GET THE GANG TOGETHER ...

...AND SEARCH ON FOOT!

PITA (HALT)
......!

ZAWA (CHATTER)
......
ZAWA

GURU (SPIN)
BA (TURN)
ZA (STEP)
ZA
...
......!
GARAAAN (EMPTY)
NOBODY... HERE?

IT DEFINITELY FEELS LIKE I'M BEING WATCHED.

MY IMAGINATION, I GUESS...

TO (TMP)

......

...

GULP.

Track 08: New Sensation

ROSE GUNS DAYS
Season2

〈...ANY CHANGES TO REPORT?〉
......

〈OR DID YOU REALLY JUST PAY ME A VISIT IN ORDER TO EAT SOME MOONCAKES...?〉
......

HISO (WHISPER)

...!

......
<WHAT COULD SHE POSSIBLY BE TRYING TO START HERE...?>

<...NO, IT'S FINE.>
<LET HER DO AS SHE PLEASES.>

<BUT NATURALLY...>
<...DON'T TAKE YOUR EYES OFF OF HER.>

CHINA-TOWN
GAYA (CHATTER)
GAYA

<OKAY, NEXT.>
<OUR AGENCY CHARGE IS $150.>
<SHIT. DAMN YOU AND YOUR KICKBACKS...>
<DON'T LIKE IT? GO SOMEWHERE ELSE!>
<GUH ...>

...UM-HUM.

LIKE WE THOUGHT. THIS IS THE PLACEMENT SCAM.
HEY!
THAT'S THE CUE-BALL BASTARD!

SO THIS IS WHERE HE'S RECRUITING WORKERS.
WHAT NOW? TAKE PICTURES FROM 'ERE!?
...HMM.

UNLESS WE CAN GET SHOTS INSIDE, IT'S NOT ENOUGH PROOF.

LET'S TRY SNEAKING IN THE BACK.

...NOPE. NOT HAP-PENING.
PORI PORI (SCRATCH)

GUY LOOKS LIKE A DOOR GUARD FOR A REASON.
IT'S ALL RUINED IF HE SEES OLIVER COMING IN TIME TO RAISE THE ALARM.
......

...WE CAN DO IT.

...!
WITH NINA'S SLING-SHOT...
...AND CHARLES' SPEED...
...AND OLIVER'S KICKS...

WE CAN OPEN A PATH...!

G—
GOT IT, DEARIE...
KYU (GRIP)

HA-HA. ...FIRST TIME FER EVERY-THING, I GUESS.

THIS THING'S FINALLY GONNA PROVE USEFUL ...!
GIRI (YANK)

...S'ONLY STRONG ENOUGH T'DISTRACT 'IM FER A SECOND...

—BUT...

...TOO BAD...

IF WE MAKE THIS A TEAM EFFORT...
KAN (PING)
!!
<EH...?>

<BRIGHT...>
<WHA...?
HYU (FWOOSH)
<WHAT THE—!?>

DO
(WHAK)
GAHHH!
DOSA
(THUD)

...WE DID IT.
WOO-HOO! JUST LIKE YEH PLANNED IT, ZEL!
WE'RE GOOD. HE'S OUT COLD.
I DIDN'T ACTUALLY DO ANY-THING...

...NO.
WITHOUT YOU, ZEL, IT WOULDN'T HAVE GONE LIKE THIS.

JUST GOES TO SHOW...

...THAT WE'RE MEANT TO BE A QUARTET ...!

GAYA (CHATTER)
GAYA

〈LISTEN UP, BOYS!〉
〈ONCE AT THE WORKSITE, DON'T GO SPEAKING CHINESE!〉
〈YOU WANNA BLEND IN WITH THE JAPANESE CROWDS!!〉
ONE, TWO, THREE ...

HEH, THIS IS GOOD... THANKS, AS ALWAYS!
NO, THANK YOU. YOU DO US A GREAT SERVICE.
HEKO (BOW)
HEKO

I GOTTA HAND IT TO YOU GOLDEN DRAGONS...
HEH HEH HEH...
So baldy's in cahoots with the Golden Dragons.
We can be sure of that much now...

Better get a snapshot...

PASHA (SNAP)

——!!
Damn. We'll be spotted.

PASHA
Good, that's enough! Let's get outta here.
Shh.
PASHA

‹WHAT'RE YOU DOING?›
‹UGHHH...›
‹SOMEONE GOT THE DROP ON YOU!?›

...!

WE NEED ANOTHER WAY OUT...
ZEL...

HOW ABOUT THAT WINDOW!?

KAN (CLANK)
WAHHH! WE'LL BE SITTIN' DUCKS FER THE GUYS OUTSIDE...
KAN
STOP OVER-THINKING IT AND CLIMB!

GU (TUG) GU GU
DOESN'T SEEM TO BE LOCKED, BUT...
...IT WON'T BUDGE AN INCH!
STOP MESSING AROUND AND GET IT OPEN.
IF WE GET CAUGHT, YER GONNA END UP AS FILLIN' FER THOSE MEAT BUNS YEH LOVE SO MUCH, CHARLES.
DON'T EVEN JOKE ABOUT THAT...

<WHAT'RE YOU DOING UP THERE?>
!?
<IT'S A COUPLE OF ROACHES. KILL 'EM!!>
JYAKI (KACHAK)

THEY JUST SAID THEY'RE GONNA KILL US...!
GUI (YANK)
MOVE IT, CHARLES.
I'LL...

...KICK IT OPEN!!

GASHISHI (SHATTER)

GAN (BLAM)

<DON'T LET THEM GET AWAY!!>

GAN

GAN (BLAM)
THEY'RE SERIOUSLY SHOOTING AT US!
JUST JUMP, CHARLES!
GAN
GAN

GAN
GAN
WE'D BETTER MAKE FOR THE MAIN STREETS.

ZA (STEP)

!?

〈IT'S THE END OF THE LINE FOR YOU BRATS!!〉

ZEL! RUN AHEAD! WE'LL BUY YOU SOME TIME.

HOW'RE YOU GONNA DO THAT!?

THESE'RE THE TACTICS YOU TAUGHT US, ZEL!

NINA!

YEP...

HAH!!

BYUN (FLIK)

‹YOUCH...›
‹OWWW!›
SHURU (PULL)

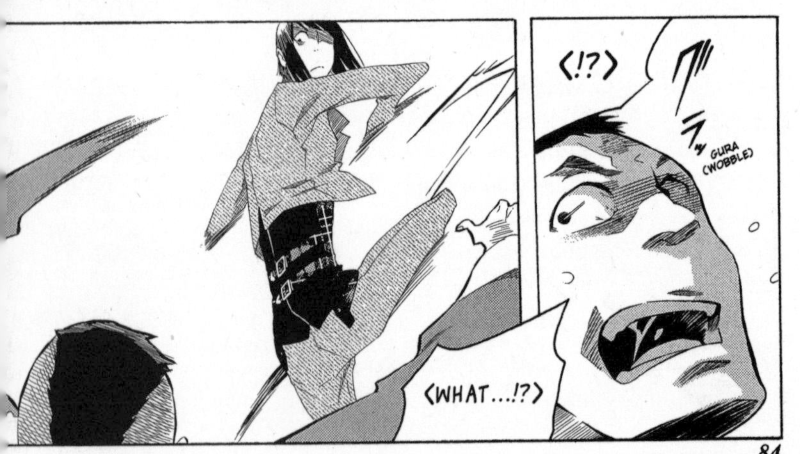
HYUN
(FWISH)
<!?>
GURA
(WOBBLE)
<WHAT...!?>

(!?)
DOKA (WHAM)
DOSA (THUD)
WOW.
...!?
ZEL...
WATCH OUT.
ZA (STEP)
HUH...

‹DON'T MOVE!!›

GA (GRAB)

...

‹TRY ME. GO ON. TAKE ONE MORE STEP...›

‹...IF YOU WANT HER DEAD!!›

ZEL ...

...WHAT DO I DO?

I HAVE TO DO SOMETHING
GOTTA DO SOMETHING.

SOME-THING...

IF YOU DON'T ACT FOR YOURSELF, YOU CAN'T SAVE ANYONE.

SO STAND UP.
...!?

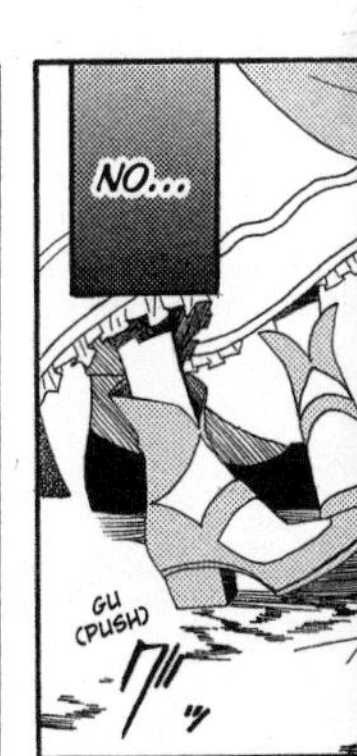
NO...
GU (PUSH)

〈I SAID, DON'T MOVE!〉
GU
GU
〈STOP LEANING BACK LIKE THAT.〉
GU
GU
GU

NO...

GUI (YANK)

FUWA (FLING)

DON'T MAKE ME REMEMBER ...!!

IT'S TOO PAINFUL.

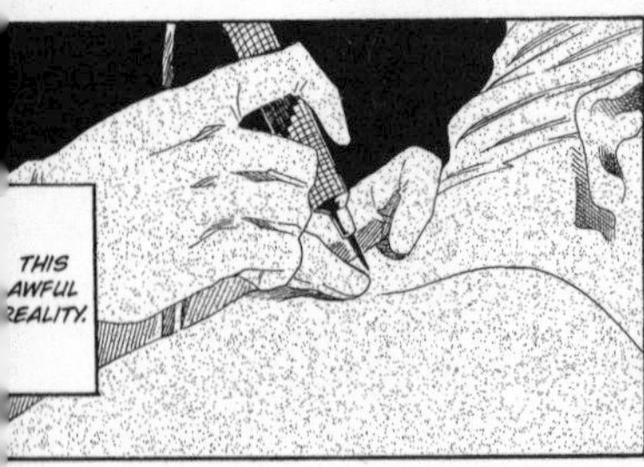
THIS AWFUL REALITY.

I...

...WON'T GET TO LAUGH AND SMILE WITH THEM ANYMORE...!

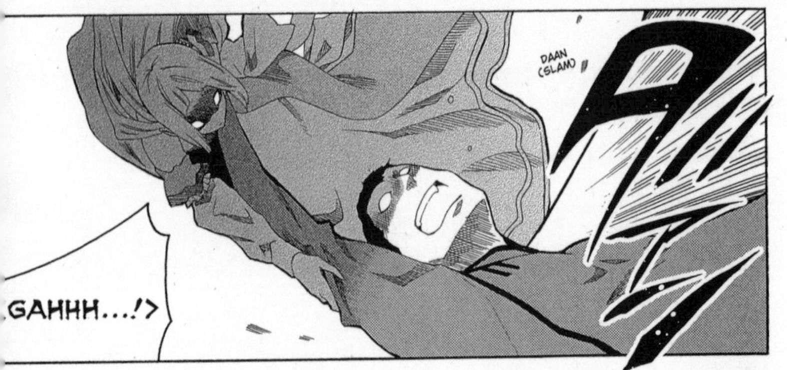
DAAN (SLAM)
GAHHH...!>

I...
I...

...!

!

KEEP GOING, ZEL!
GUI (TUG)
...

LOOK AT YO ZEL!
WHAT WAS THAT? JUDO!?
......

I'M NOT SURE. ACTU ALLY
I CAN'T TELL THEM.
IT JUST HAPPENED ...

YOUR MEMORIES MIGHT BE GONE, BUT THE BODY ALWAYS REMEMBERS.
HYAHHH!

YER QUITE A GAL, ZEL.
I REMEMBER EVERYTHING.

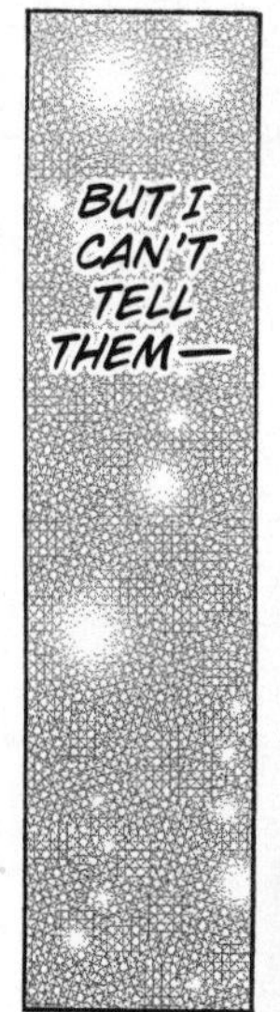
BUT I CAN'T TELL THEM—

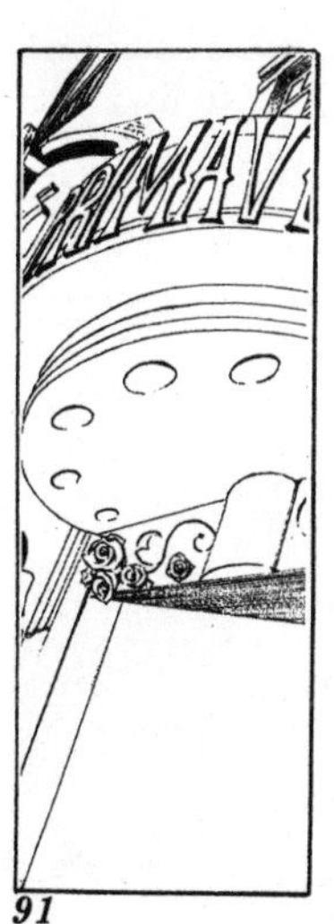

OOH. LOOKIT THIS...

WE GOT 'EM DEAD TO RIGHTS.
PIRA (FLIP)

GUY ON THE LEFT IS SEISHOU SOU...AN OFFICER OF THE GOLDEN DRAGONS.
AND BALDY IS THE HEAD OF THE SHIPPING UNION.
WELL DONE WITH THIS, WAYNE.
...

IT WAS SOME OF THE YOUNGSTERS IN MY CREW.
THEY WENT A LITTLE OVERBOARD...

ROSE... THIS IS OUR REALITY.
NOBLE INTENTIONS LIKE YOURS RARELY PAN OUT IN THE UNDERWORLD.

...DOES THIS MAN...
...WORK UNDER MEIJIU-SAN...?

MEIJIU LEE IS THE BOSS OF SMALL LOC CHINATOWN.
IT'S UNLIKELY HE WOULDN'T KNOW ABOUT BUSINESS GOING ON AT HIS DOORSTEP.
DON'T YOU THINK...?
...

...I UNDER STAN
LET'S PAY MEIJIU-SAN A VISIT...
HOPEFULLY WE CAN TAKE CARE OF THIS WITHOUT WOUNDING HIS PRIDE TOO MUCH.

WE'RE.
...GOING TO ANNOUNCE THE FORMATION OF THE DISTRICT 23 JAPANESE WORKERS' UNION.

Immigrant Song

...WHO TOLD YOU TO GO AND RISK YOUR NECKS LIKE THIS?
WITHOUT EVEN TELLING ME FIRST?

SORRY, BIG BRO ...!
WE JUST WANTED T'BE USEFUL T'YEH, BIG BRO WAYNE.
WE AD T'DO SOME- HING...!

ACTU- ALLY, I...
WE ALL DECIDED TOGETH- ER!

RAPUN- ZEL.
YOU'RE A GUEST HERE.
NOT ONE OF THE WILD DOGS.

EVEN IF SHE ISN'T...
...SHE'S STILL OUR PAL.
...

...IF THEY'D TOLD YOU...
.WOULD YOU HAVE LET THEM DO IT?

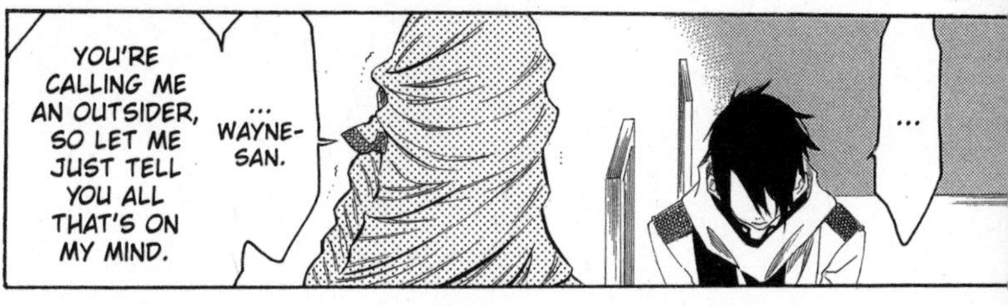
...
... WAYNE-SAN.
YOU'RE CALLING ME AN OUTSIDER, SO LET ME JUST TELL YOU ALL THAT'S ON MY MIND.

YOU OUGHT TO KNOW THESE THREE AREN'T THE "DUNCES" OF THE WILD DOGS.
THEY'RE YOUNG WOLVES!
AND THEY WANT TO BE JUST LIKE YOU...!

CAN'T YOU HONOR THEIR PASSION, SOMEHOW?
DOESN'T IT MOVE YOU?
THEY'D BRAVE ANY DANGER FOR YOUR SAKE...!
THE ONLY THING THEY FEAR...

TO THEM... YOU'RE EVERYTHING!!

...IS YOUR REJECTION!
NOT EARNING YOUR RESPECT!

... OLIVER.
WHAT RAPUNZEL JUST SAID—IS THAT HOW YOU ALL REALLY FEEL?
...!

...YES.

WE'RE WILD DOGS...
...WE WANT TO LIVE AS PROUD WOLVES...
...JUST LIKE YOU, BIG BRO WAYNE...

...

SIGH.
...THE WILD DOGS...
...ARE A PACK OF WOLVES THAT FOL-LOW THEIR LEADER.

IF YOU CAN'T GO WITH THE PACK...
...THEN I CAN'T HAVE YOU IN THE WILD DOGS.

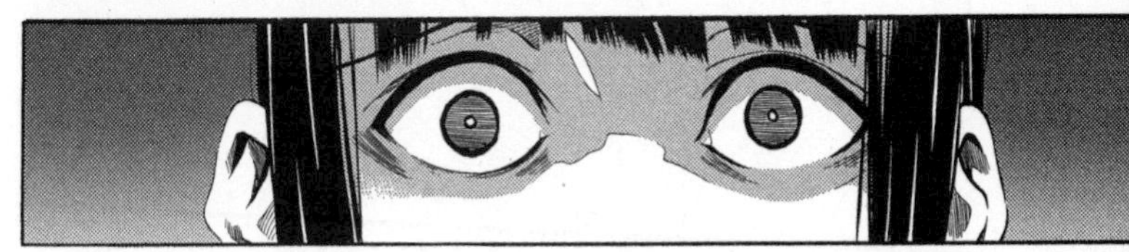

...AH.

...We're gettin' kicked out... of the group?

IT'S FINE, ZEL!
WAYNE-SAN...!

NO... IT'S NOT!!
HOW CAN YOU BE FINE WITH THIS!?

WAYNE-SAN'S ALREADY DECIDED.
AND WE WERE WOLVES, IF ONLY FOR A MOMENT.

It's fine...

OLI-VER...

YOU CAN'T BE WILD DOGS IF YOU DON'T STICK TO THE PACK, SO...

...BE ROAMING WOLVES.
THE WANDERING DOGS!

...HUH?

GI (CREAK)
THAT'S WHAT I'LL CALL YOU FOUR, STARTING TODAY.
YOU'RE FREE TO TRY WHATEVER HAREBRAINED SCHEMES YOU WANT.
JUST BE SURE TO TELL ME, YOUR BOSS, FIRST.

...ZEL.
ROSE-SAN TOLD ME TO LET YOU DO AS YOU PLEASE.
SO IF YOU WANT TO LIVE AS A WOLF, I'VE GOT NO RIGHT TO STOP YOU...

SO HOW ABOUT YOU...
...CALL ME BOSS?

...YES, BOSS!

...GOT IT.
SINCE YOU'RE WANDERING DOGS NOW, YOU'LL HAVE TO DRIFT AROUND THE CITY.
GACHI (CLICK)
BE MY EYES AND EARS OUT THERE.

I'M EXPECTING BIG THINGS FROM YOU GUYS!

PATAN (CLOSE)
パタン…

WE...

YEAHHH!

WE DID IT!!

WE'RE THE WANDERING DOGS NOW...

THE WANDERING DOGS!

S'LIKE A SECRET SQUAD, JUST FER US!
I'VE BEEN WAITING FOR THIS DAY...
I FEEL LIKE... I'M ON FIRE!!

POTATA (DRIP)
ZEL ...?
WHAT?
WHAT'S WRONG !?

Noth-ing...
Just so happy ...
I'M SORRY, EVERYONE.

I'M SORRY.
ZAA (WHOOSH)

I...
I CAN'T...
...BE YOUR FRIEND...
GUSU (SNIFFLE)
UGH...
HIC.
Hey now, stop all that blubbering.

CHIRIN (JANGLE)

TOUTO NEWS
JAPANESE IN DISTRICT 23 TO RECEIVE CERTIFICATES OF RESIDENCE
DISTRICT 23 JAPANESE WORKERS' UNION
NEWLY FORMED JAPANESE WORKERS' UNION!
SPECIAL EDITION!

Track 09: Standing in the Dark

SO WORKERS NEED TO BE REGISTERED AS JAPANESE CITIZENS TO JOIN THE UNION...
THEY'VE GOTTA HAVE THESE CERTIFICATES OF RESIDENCE PROVING THEY'VE LIVED IN DISTRICT 23 FOR AT LEAST A YEAR...
THIS MEANS OUTSIDERS WON'T BE STEALING THOSE JOBS ANYMORE!

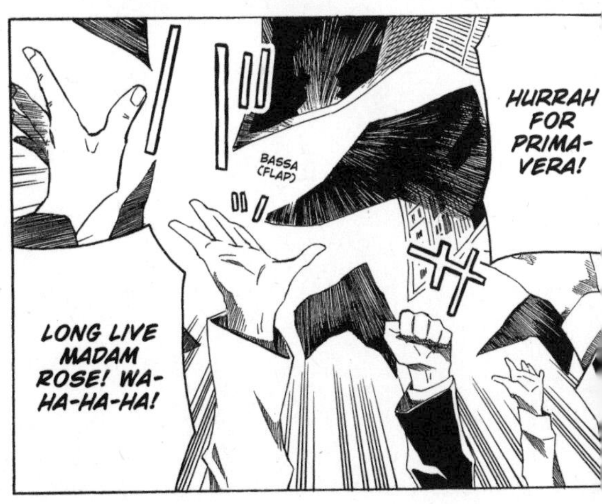
HURRAH FOR PRIMA-VERA!
BASSA (FLAP)
LONG LIVE MADAM ROSE! WA-HA-HA-HA!

DOTA (STOMP)
DOTA
DOTA

US WANDER-ING DOGS...

BAN (BAM)
HEY, GUYS— BIG NEWS!

...PA...

...HAVE BEEN INVITED TO MADAM ROSE'S PASTA PARTY!
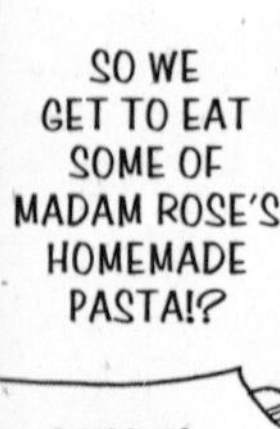

THE PASTA PARTY —!!?
SO WE GET TO EAT SOME OF MADAM ROSE'S HOMEMADE PASTA!?
IDIOT! THAT'S NOT WHAT IT MEANS.

MADAM ROSE'LL BE THERE OF COURSE.
PLUS THE GRAND BOSS AND CONSI-GLIERE...
IT'S AN EVENT FOR ALL THE BOSSES OF PRIMAVERA'S CREWS...!

IT'S OUR CHANCE TO MAKE OUR FACES KNOWN!
AMAZING!!

AND S'ALL THANKS T'ZEL, HERE.
THANKS T'THAT BUSINESS WITH THE PLACEMENT SCAM.
GYUUU (HUG)
THANKS, ZEL!
......

I REALLY...
...DIDN'T DO MUCH...

CHINA-TOWN

BAN (SLAM)

<HELLOOOO MY TTLE MEI. YOU MUST BE HAPPY!!>

<...SIR.>

SO HAS THE ELDER COUNCIL TRULY SENT AN ASSASSIN AFTER ME...?
THIS MAN IS ANOTHER HIGH-RANKING OFFICER WITH THE TITLE "DRAGON."

THE AZURE DRAGON KING—YUANHONG WANG ...!
BASA (FLAP)
<DID YOU SEE THE SPECIAL EDITION?>

〈THIS WON'T DOOO...! PRIMAVERA'S PUSHED THEIR LUCK TOO FAR THIS TIME!〉
NA HA HA!
〈THE ELDER COUNCIL IS HOPPING MAD!!〉
〈ON THE OTHER HAND, I WAS NEARLY IN A POSITION TO MAKE A DEAL FOR THE EXCLUSIVITY RIGHTS IN DISTRICT 23...〉

PI (FLIP)
〈OHH?〉
〈BUT ONE OF YOUR LACKEYS DECIDED TO ENGAGE IN SOME SIDE BUSINESS...〉

〈I SEEM TO REMEMBER...〉
〈...SOU BEING ONE OF YOURS, NO...?〉

POI (TOSS)
〈LITTLE SOU? EXCLUSIVITY RIGHTS?
〈WHAT ON EARTH ARE YOU TALKING ABOUT?〉
〈......〉
〈ALL THAT MATTERS NOW IS THAT THE DISCONTENTMENT OF THE DISTRICT 22 LABORERS IS ABOUT TO COME TO A HEAD...〉
〈THEY'RE DEMANDING WORK FOR THE SAME HIGH WAGES THAT PRIMAVERA IS PROVIDING!〉

〈...IF WE WERE TRULY OF A MIND TO MAKE THAT HAPPEN...〉
〈...WE COULD VERY EASILY GUARANTEE SUCH WAGES FOR OUR COUNTRYMEN... USING OUR OWN EXCLUSIVITY RIGHTS.〉

‹THE ELDER COUNCIL WOULD NEVER ALLOW THAT.›
‹IF WE INCREASED WAGES, AS PRIMAVERA HAS...›
‹...THE ELDERS' SHARE WOULD TAKE A SERIOUS HIT.›

‹PLEASE LEAVE THIS TO ME.›
‹I WILL RESOLVE THE ISSUE... IN A WAY THAT PLEASES THE ELDERS.›

‹I'LL HAVE TO MAKE MADAM ROSE REMEMBER...›

‹...THAT JAPAN WAS VANQUISHED.›

‹AND ITS PEOPLE NLY LIVE ON THANKS TO THE MERCY AND MAGNANIMITY OF OTHERS.›

MILLENN-
IUM
RESTAU-
RANT

YAHOO, MADAM ROSE.
WELCOME TO MY CASTLE!
BAN (BAM)

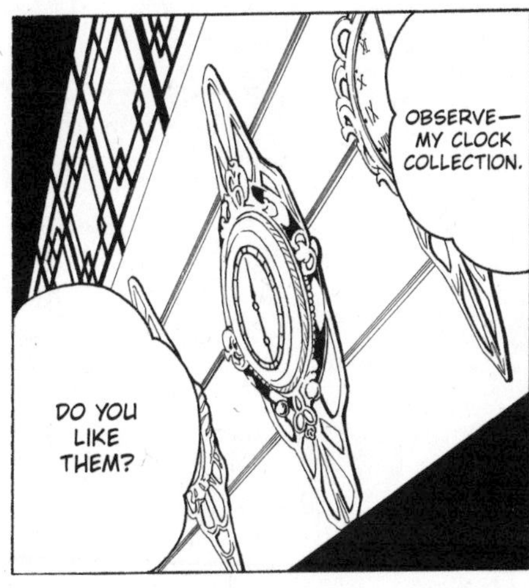
OBSERVE—MY CLOCK COLLECTION.
DO YOU LIKE THEM?

YOU SPEAK JAPANESE QUITE WELL...
...MR. WANG.

IT'S A BEAUTIFUL COLLECTION.
YOU MUST REALLY VALUE YOUR TIME...

...AS DO WE...

TO GET RIGHT TO IT, THERE'S ONLY ONE REASON YOU'RE HERE TODAY.
YOU WISH TO ENSURE CONTINUED FRIENDSHIP BETWEEN THE CHINESE AND JAPANESE!

BUT T GOLD DRAGO AND PRIMA VERA

... ALREA HAVE FRIEND WORKI RELATIO SHIP

YES, BUT!

THAT FRIENDSHIP HANGS IN THE BALANCE THANKS TO YOUR JAPANESE WORKERS' UNION.

TO DEAL WITH THIS PROBLEM...

...THE ELDER COUNCIL THINKS WE SHOULD DECLARE WAR ON PRIMAVERA!!

!

ALL OF DISTRIC 22 IS IN PANIC!
THE WORKERS ARE RIOTING, DEMANDING THE SAME PAY PRIMAVERA OFFERS...
WE'RE EXPERI-ENCING BOYCOTTS. SABOTAGE, EVEN...
THEIR DEMONSTRATIONS ARE GETTING OUT OF HAND!!

THEIR FAITH IN OUR ABILITY TO MAINTAIN A STABLE CHINATOWN IS WANING...
...AND YOU ARE RESPONSIBLE FOR THAT!

YOU DON'T THINK YOU'RE RESPONSIBLE FOR ANY OF IT...?

NOT AT ALL!
WE'RE READY TO FIRE BACK AGAINST PRIMAVERA'S ONE-SIDED ECONOMIC CHALLENGE.
WE HAVE A DUTY TO PROTECT OUR BRETHREN.

...
GACHAN (CLATTER)

GA (GRAB)
AT THIS RATE, THERE'LL BE WAR!
BUT NEITHER OF US WANTS THAT, RIGHT!?
IT WOULD BE TRAGIC!
...

...IS THAT A THREAT?

GU (PRESS)
GU
DON'T MIS-UNDER-STAND.
I'M HERE TODAY AS AN EMISSARY OF PEACE.

IF YOU'RE WILLING TO COMPROMISE ...
...EVEN THE ELDER COUNCIL MAY BE PACIFIED...

COMPRO-MISE...?

GO ON, MEI-CHAN!

PACHIN (SNAP)

...I WILL NOW STATE THE ELDER COUNCIL'S DEMANDS.

FIRST, RETURN THE EXTRAVAGANT LABOR WAGES TO THE STANDARDS OF LAST YEAR.

SECOND, AS PROOF OF OUR FRIENDSHIP...

...GRANT US ONE-THIRD OF THE EXCLUSIVITY RIGHTS FOR DISTRICT 23.

HOW DARE YOU MAKE SUCH A BRAZEN ...

THIS IS BEYOND UNREASON-ABLE...!
GATA (SLAM)

CALM DOWN, RICHARD-KUN.
DON'T LET THEM GET YOU RILED UP.

I CAN'T GIVE YOU AN IMMEDIATE RESPONSE.
FIRST WE NEED TO GATHER OUR THOUGHTS.
YOU'LL HAVE YOUR ANSWER IN A FEW DAYS' TIME.
...NO MATTER YOUR ESPONSE ...

...ARE YOU PREPARED FOR ANY CON-SEQUENCES...
...TO BE ENTIRELY ON YOUR HEAD...?

I'VE ALWAYS MADE A POINT OF TAKING RESPONSI-BILITY...
...FOR MY ECISIONS.
KOTSU (CLICK)

...BE-
CAUSE,
WANG-
SAN...
...WHERE YOU REFUSE TO TAKE THE SMALLEST RESPONSIBILITY FOR ANYTHING...
...I AM QUITE DIFFERENT.
GOKU (GULP)

GYURURURU (SPIN)
BURORO (VROOM)
〈...I SEE NOW, LITTLE MEI.〉
〈MY TRUE ENEMY IS MADAM ROSE.〉
〈...IF WE *LET ANYONE LIVE*, IT SHOULD BE RICHARD.〉

〈...DID YOU JUST SAY, "LET ANYONE LIVE"?〉

〈WE WILL REMOVE MADAM ROSE FROM THE PICTURE!〉
〈...AND USE "HOTARUBI" TO DO IT.〉

〈ONCE PRIMAVERA IS STRIPPED OF ITS CHARISMATIC LEADER...〉
〈...THE SHORT-TEMPERED RICHARD WON'T BE ABLE TO HOLD IT TOGETHER.〉
〈PRIMAVERA WILL SELF-DESTRUCT, NO NEED FOR ANY BATTLES...〉

...
〈FOR SHE IS THE ELDERS' PRIZED PET...〉
〈THOUGH ...〉

〈...I STILL HAVEN'T HAD THE PLEASURE OF MEETING HER, MYSELF.〉
〈NA-HA-HA-HA-HA!!〉
FURA (DRIFT)

DON (BUMP)
〈HEY! WATCH WHERE YOU'RE GOING.〉
〈...〉

〈I'M SORRY...〉

KO (TAK)

〈...I'M HOTARUBI.〉
〈IS XIAO-LAN HERE?〉

HYURURU
(WHOOSH)

<...YOU'VE COME.>
TO
(TMP)

<YOU DIDN'T SHOW UP LAST MONTH.>

<...I'VE BEEN ON THE JOB.>

<SO JUST RELAX.>

GASHAN
(CLACK)

<THIS WAY.>

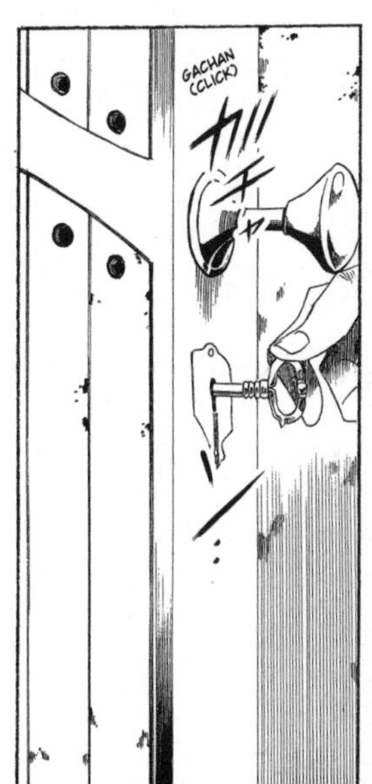
GACHAN
(CLICK)

GII
(CREAK)

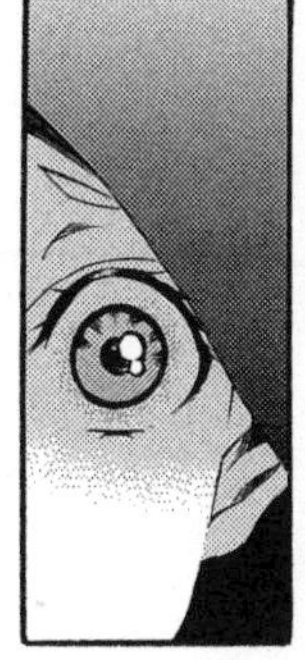

...!
DA
(DASH)

DADDY....!

DON
(BAM)
I'm so sorry, Daddy...
I'm sorry I couldn't come to see you.
HOTARU...
I'M JUST GLAD YOU'RE SAFE.
<...PARDON OUR PRESENCE.>
<WE'LL LEAVE YOU ALONE FOR A MOMENT...>

<THE GOLDEN DRAGONS ARE GRATEFUL FOR YOUR EXCELLENT WORK.>
<KEEP IT UP AND WE WILL CONTINUE TO PROTECT YOUR FATHER FROM THE POLICE.>

GIII (CREAK)

BATAN (CLOSE)
...

PAN (SLAP)

DOSA (THUD)

...!

YOU FOOL!!

WHY DIDN'T YOU JUST LEAVE ME AND MAKE A RUN FOR IT!?

NO FATHER WOULD WANT HIS DAUGHTER TO DIRTY HER HANDS SO THAT HE COULD LIVE...!

NO GOOD FATHER WOULD DO SO...

...IT'S OKAY.

I'M ONLY A SPY THIS TIME...

...HO-TARU.

I DON'T WANT YOU EVER COMING BACK HERE.

FROM TODAY ON, JUST FORGET ABOUT ME.

PATA (DRIP)
PATA
...DON'T SAY THAT.

MOTHER, BIG SIS...
THEY'RE ALL DEAD...
THE BOYS ...

IF I STOP DOING THIS WORK ...
...I'LL LOSE MY FATHER TOO...

I can't let you die, Daddy...
I'd have no reason to go on...
Uhhh...

UWAAAAAAAH...
HO-TARU ...

ZAAAAA (FSSSHHH)

PICHA (SPLISH)

PICHA

PICHA
......

Immigrant
!

PASHA (SPLASH)
PASHA
PACHAN (SPLOSH)

ZEL!

THAT'S YOU, RIGHT, ZEL?

WHERE'D YOU RUN TO? AND WITHOUT AN UMBRELLA ...?

... CHARLES.

NOT EVEN A NOTE? WE WERE WORRIED SICK...
AND NOW YER SOAKED T'THE BONE!
BATA (STOMP)
BATA
BATA

BAN
(SLAM)

ZEL...!

WE WERE WOR-RIED!
DOKA (STEP)
DOKA
YOU WERE ACTING WEIRD, AND THEN...

DID SOMETHING 'APPEN...?

......
JUST SOME BUSINESS THAT RAN LATE...
... SORRY.

ZEL.
YOU REALLY TRUST US THAT LITTLE!?

BUSI-NESS ...?

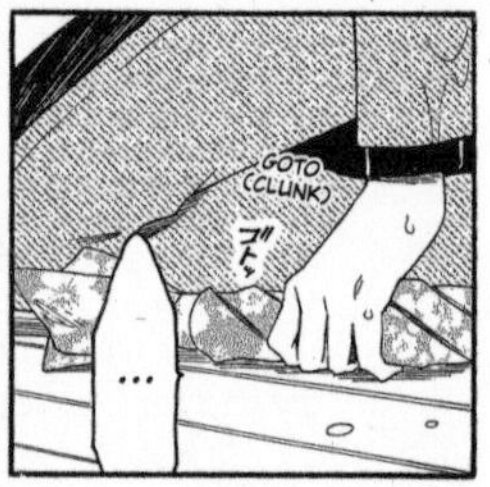
GOTO (CLUNK)
ゴトッ
...

...!
I...
I'M YOUR ALLY, ZEL, WHATEVER THE CASE!

SO IS NINA...

...AND CHARLES!

WE OWE YOU SO MUCH...!
SO...

...JUST TELL US WHAT'S WRONG.

...SORRY, OLIVER.

...I...
...NEED TO DRY MY HAIR.

... STARTING TOMOR-ROW...
...EVERY-THING WILL BE BACK TO NORMAL.

THIS PATHETIC VERSION OF ME RIGHT NOW? JUST FORGET ABOUT HER...

GII (CREAK)

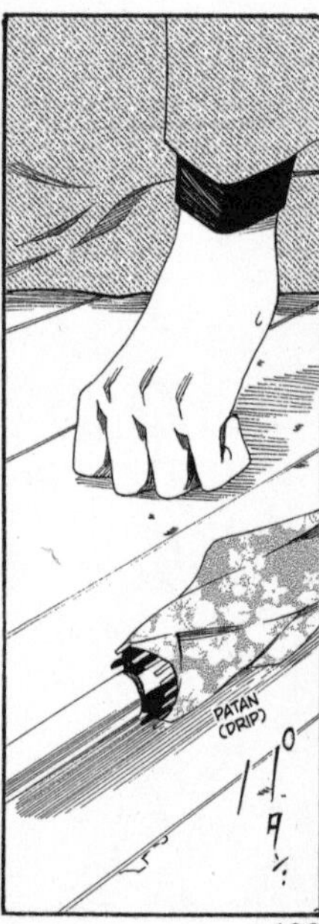

PATAN (DRIP)

—...
... ZEL ...

I THINK.
...HER MEMORIES MIGHT HAVE RETURNED...

...OH.
MUST 'AVE SOMETHING T'DO WITH THAT...
HUH?

WHAT'S "THAT"!?
THE TATTOO BEHIND HER NECK.

YOU SAW IT, RIGHT?
BACK WHEN SHE TOSSED THAT GOLDEN DRAGON THUG...

'ARD TO IMAGINE THAT ZEL WOULD GO...
...'N' GET A CREEPY TATTOO LIKE THAT ALL ON 'ER OWN.
......

OH, ZEL...

...STILL, WHATEVER'S GOING ON...
...SHE CAME BACK TO US...

KACHI (TICK)
KOCHI (TOCK)

SUUU (ZZZ)
MUKU (RISE)

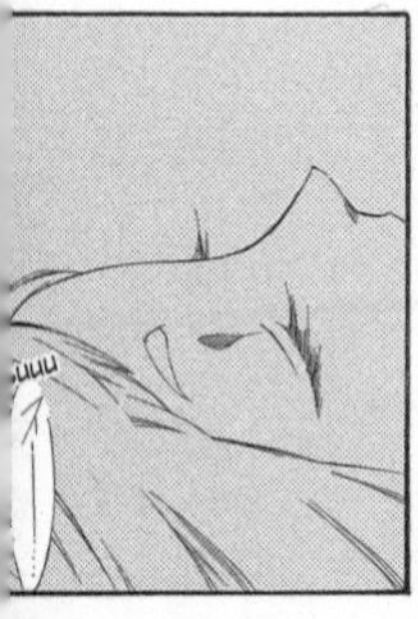

...

もぞ…
MOZO (SNUGGLE)

…スー
SUUU

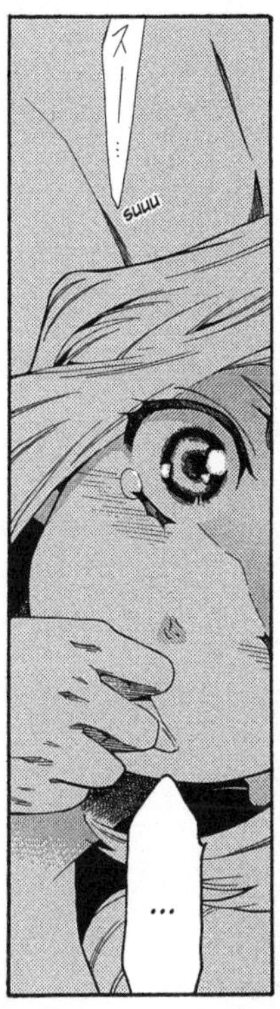

スー…
SUUU
…

POROポロ…
(DRIP)
(...AT LAST.)
(SO THEY'RE CALLING IT THE "PASTA PARTY.")
(VERY WELL DONE, INDEED.)
(...THANK YOU...)
(...VERY MUCH...)

(I WAS TOLD TO GIVE YOU THIS POISON TO USE.)
SU (PUSH)
(FLAVORLESS. ODORLESS...)
SARA (FSSHH)
(THE TARGET...)
SARA
PACHIN (CLICK)
(A SMALL DOSE IS ENOUGH TO CAUSE CARDIAC ARREST AND DEATH ONE WEEK AFTER INGESTION.)

〈...IS PRIMAVERA'S LEADER.〉
〈ROSE HAIBARA.〉
〈...UNDERSTOOD?〉
〈HOTARUBI?〉

〈...YES.〉

ZAAA (FSSSHHH)
<...WHAT AN AWFUL RAIN.>
<IT STILL SHOWS NO SIGN OF STOPPING.>

Track 10: If I Could Fly

...!

......
<HOTARUBI'S BEEN SET IN MOTION.>
<WITHIN TEN DAYS' TIME, MADAM ROSE WILL NO LONGER BE IN OUR WAY...>

〈AFTER THAT, ONCE RICHARD BECOMES THEIR LEADER...〉
〈...WE WILL NEED TO SIMPLY CONVINCE HIM THAT ALLYING WITH THE GOLDEN DRAGONS IS HIS BEST OPTION.〉
〈FOR THAT, WE NEED A SCAPEGOAT.〉
〈...A SCAPEGOAT?〉
〈HE DOESN'T HAVE THE CHARISMA TO KEEP PRIMAVERA UNIFIED.〉
〈CHARISMA IN THE UNDERWORLD IS ALL ABOUT HEROISM. CHIVALRY. ROMANCE...DO YOU UNDERSTAND, LITTLE MEI?〉
ZAAA (FSSSHHH)
〈...I SEE. SO WE SOMEHOW GIVE RICHARD A CHANCE TO BE HEROIC, THEREBY ALLOWING FOR RECONCILIATION.〉
E WILL PREPARE SOMEONE FROM THE NESE SIDE TO "LOSE" TO RICHARD.〉
〈BECAUSE EXCLUSIVITY RIGHTS TAKEN BY FORCE ARE QUITE DIFFERENT THAN THOSE HANDED OVER WILLINGLY!〉
〈...BUT...〉
〈WE NEED ONE IMPORTANT ENOUGH TO WIN OVER PRIMAVERA, WHICH ESSENTIALLY CONTROLS ALL OF DISTRICT 23...〉
〈WHOSE HEAD HAS TO ROLL FOR THAT...?〉

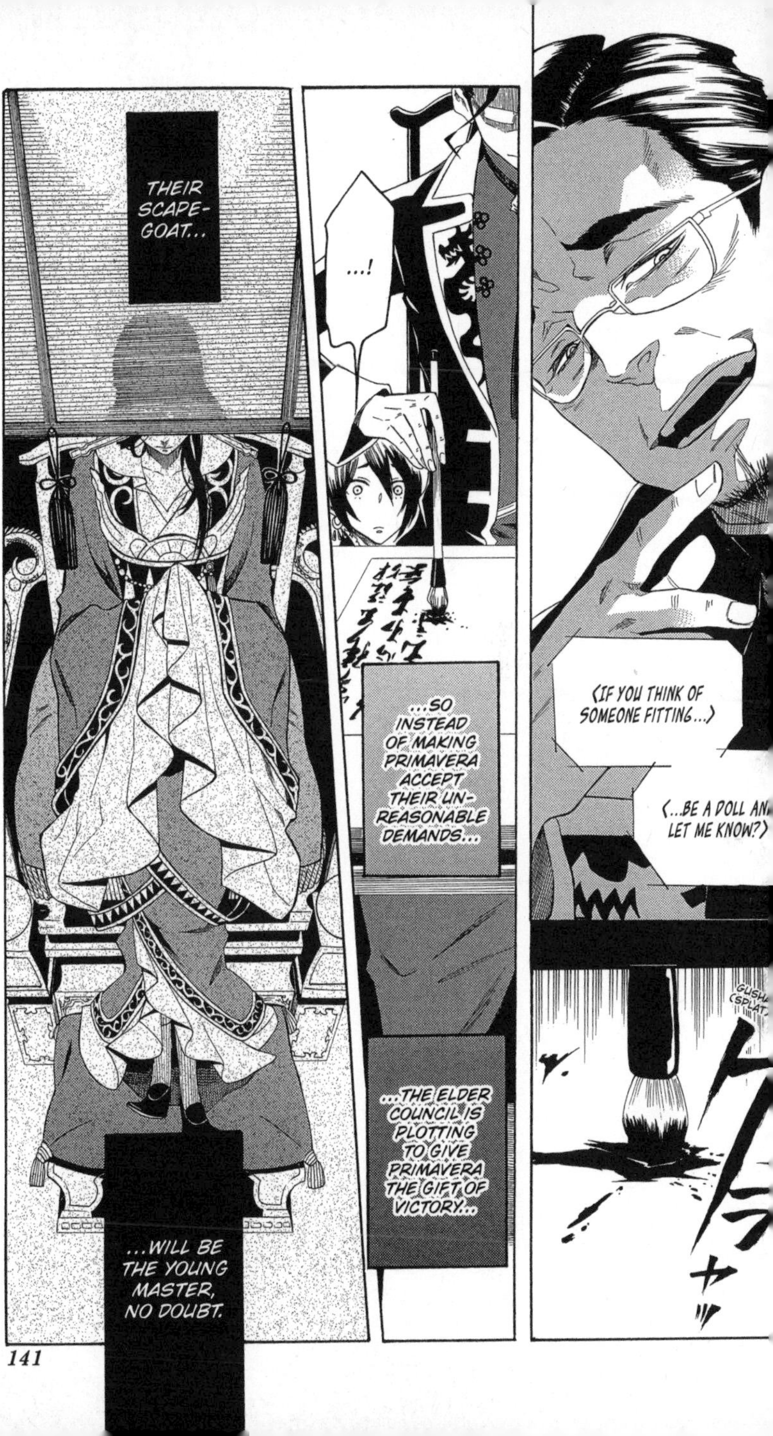

〈IF YOU THINK OF SOMEONE FITTING...〉
〈...BE A DOLL AN
LET ME KNOW?〉
GUSH
(SPLAT

...!

...SO INSTEAD OF MAKING PRIMAVERA ACCEPT THEIR UN-REASONABLE DEMANDS...

...THE ELDER COUNCIL IS PLOTTING TO GIVE PRIMAVERA THE GIFT OF VICTORY...

THEIR SCAPE-GOAT...

...WILL BE THE YOUNG MASTER, NO DOUBT.

THE SON OF OUR FALLEN FORMER LEADER WILL BE THEIR SACRIFICE.
THEY'RE PLANNING TO SEIZE COMPLETE CONTROL OF THE GOLDEN DRAGONS...
...ALL OUT OF PURE SELF-INTEREST.

<THOSE DESPICABLE, SENILE OLD FOOLS...>

<I, BLACK DRAGON LEE... WILL GLADLY HAVE MY OWN NAME DRAGGED THROUGH THE MUD...>

<...BUT YOU WON'T TOUCH ONE HAIR ON THE YOUNG MASTER'S HEAD!!>

POTA (DRIP)

ZAAA (FSSSHHH)
Immigrant Song
COME ON, GUYS.
WAKE UP, WAKE UP!

TODAY'S MADAM ROSE'S PASTA PARTY, ISN'T IT?
Whaa ...?
IT'S YOUR BIG CHANCE TO SHOW WHO YOU ARE TO PRIMAVERA'S TOP OFFICERS, RIGHT!?

WHOOPS ...!
SUTO (LAND)
ZEL!

ARE YOU ...
ARE YOU OKAY !?

...
...PFFT!

AH-HA-HA! HOW ABOUT YOU, WITH THOSE DARK RINGS UNDER YOUR EYES?
...
TOO NERVOUS? COULDN'T SLEEP, HUH?

ZEL...
HMM...WE'LL HAVE TO FILL THIS ONE'S STOMACH BEFORE WE GO ANYWHERE, WON'T WE?
......
...AH.
I'LL WHIP UP SOME FRIED EGGS.
PATA (TMP)
PATA
PATA

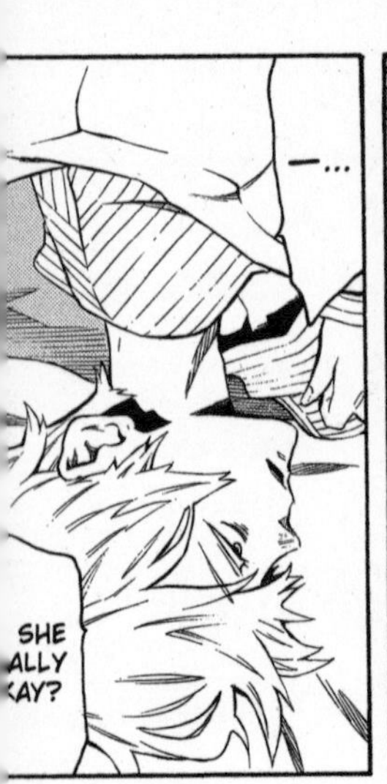
—...
SHE
ALLY
KAY?

...WHAT-EVER HER MOOD...
...ZEL IS ZEL.
IT'S ENOUGH THAT SHE'S STILL HERE WITH US.

BOOK: HOW TO CHEER SOMEONE UP

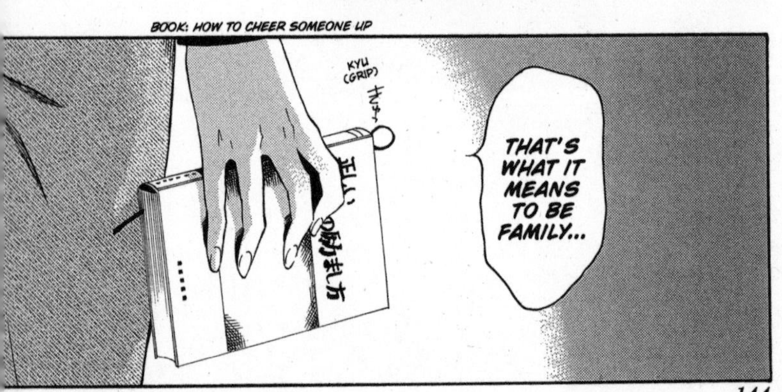
KYU (GRIP)
THAT'S WHAT IT MEANS TO BE FAMILY...

ZAAA (FSSSHHH)
WAH-HA-HA!

WHAT A RECEPTION HUH!?
S'LIKE WE'RE THE HEROES OF THIS TOWN!!
DON'T GET COCKY.
THE ONLY HERO IS THE MADAM.
INDEED.

THANK YOU FOR COMING, EVERYONE!
I HAVEN'T FORGOTTEN HOW GRATEFUL I AM TO ALL OF YOU!

WE ARE THE RESIDENTS OF THE UNDER-WORLD...
THOUGH IT MIGHT SCARE PEOPLE AND KEEP THEM AT A DISTANCE, WE MAY NEED TO FIGHT ONCE MORE...
...TO PROTECT OUR COUNTRY-MEN...

EITHER WAY, FOR THE SAKE OF PRIMAVERA AND OUR FELLOW JAPANESE...
...PLEASE CONTINUE TO LEND US YOUR SUPPORT!
YEAHHH!

HERE'S TO THE HEALTH OF PRIMAVERA!
...To health.
Madam Rose...

CARE FOR A DRINK?
I'LL HAVE SOME.
YOU'VE REALLY GOT THIS GIG DOWN, HUH?
IF YOU EVER GET SICK OF WAYNE, FEEL FREE TO JOIN ME AND MINE!
STOP TRYING TO STEAL MEMBERS OF MY CREW...
...OH?
WHERE ARE THE OTHER THREE?
WELL ...
KOCHIIN (STUNNED)
コチーーーーン...

Hey... That's the boss of Battalion, Morris Monobe-san.
And right next to him is James Tomitake-san, who leads Rich Bamboo...
Eek. 'Ardly feels like the place t'go self-promotin'.

DON'T FALTER NOW, WANDERI DOGS!
LET'S FOLLOW ZEL'S LEAD AND SERVE SOME DRINKS...

SURU (SLIP)
...Hey, mister. ♡

Can I get a refill ...?
Ooh, I've found a little boy. ♡
EH!?

You lads mu be new aroun here.
HOW OLD ARE YOU?
'OW 'BOUT THE REST OF YA? MORE BOOZE? ...OOPS— SORRY.
YAKEEE (FLASH)
HOW WOULD YOU LIKE SOME MORE REFRESH-MENTS!?
MY, MY...

W-WE'RE PLENTY RELAXED, WE ARE. SHANK YOU KINDLY, MA'AM!
ORRY, 'E'RE ALL ST A BIT RVOUS...
WHAT THE 'ELL SORTA ACCENT IS THAT?
HA HA HA.

SORRY, YOU GUYS. DIDN'T MEAN TO LEAVE YOU ON YOUR OWN...!
SHOULD WE CHANGE ROOMS, PERHAPS? THEY'RE HAVING TROUBLE RELAXING HERE.

IF A LITTLE SHINDIG GETS YOU THIS NERVOUS THOUGH...
SARA (SMOOTHLY)
...WON'T IT BE HARD FOR YOU TO SERVE AS MADAM ROSE'S BODY-GUARDS?

...!?

ADAM OSE'S ...?

BODY-
GUARDS
...!!?
DOKAN
(SHOCK)
ドカーン
CLUB PRIMAVE

...LET'S DO THIS PROPERLY, NOW.

HOW WOULD YOU GUYS...
...LIKE TO BE MY BODYGUARD TEAM?

THE MADAM I A LADY.
IT'S NOT PROPER FOR HER TO ALWAYS BE WITH A MALE BODYGUARD.
A TEAM WITH FEMALE MEMBERS ...
...AND SHARP SENSES...
...THAT WORKS WELL TOGETHER WOULD BE BEST, IN FACT.

I THINK THE WANDERING DOGS MEET ALL THOSE REQUIREMENTS.
YOU PROVED THAT WITH YOUR WORK ON THE PLACEMENT SCAM.

...YES.
I SWEAR WE'LL DO OUR DAMNDEST...!

BUNCHA STREET URCHINS LIKE US...
...WE WERE SHUNNED JUST FOR TRYING TO SURVIVE...

...I'M SO GLAD TO BE ALIVE.
WE'RE READY TO GIVE OUR EVERYTHING TO YOU!!
...

THEIR REAMS WILL EVER OME RUE.

THEY'LL NEVER BE REALIZED ...
...BECAUSE, MADAM ROSE IS GOING TO—...

WITH THIS POISON —...

IF YOU MY BOD GUARDS
...THAT MEANS DIVIN INTO THE LI OF FIRE TO PROTECT M
...SO I OWE IT TO YOU TO EXPLAIN...

...WHY I CAN'T DIE JUST YET.

...I BELIEVE...

...THAT THE JAPANESE...

...ARE A PARTICULARLY LETHARGIC PEOPLE.

...!?

...
EH?
YES, THE JAPANESE ARE IDLE...

WE RELY ON THE GOODWILL OF OTHERS TO PROTECT OURSELVES.
SOLATIONISM ND THE SEA EPT US SAFE. HEY ALLOWED S TO INDULGE N APATHY...
...LIKE A SMALL CHILD AT PLAY.

MEANWHILE, THE OTHER NATIONS OF THIS WORLD HAD TO SURVIVE BY WORKING HARD AT FOREIGN RELATIONS.

WE WILL BE BURIED BY IMMIGRANTS FROM THOSE OTHER COUNTRIES.

AND THE JAPANESE WILL BE ESTROYED.

SO UNTIL THE JAPANESE CAN LEARN TO FLOURISH ALONGSIDE OTHER PEOPLE...
...I CANNOT DIE.
I CAN'T LET MYSELF DIE!
EVEN NOW, OUR CULTURE IS ALL BUT LOST.
THE FOREIGN SENSIBILITIES WE WITNESS EVERY DAY ARE A GIVEN...
...BUT THINK BACK. TRY TO REMEMBER!
REMEMBER NEW YEAR'S WITH YOUR FAMILY. OR HINA MATSURI...
OR TANABATA IN THE SUMMER ...
REMEMBER MOON-VIEWING IN THE FALL!?

WE ONCE SAT AMIDST ALL THAT CULTURE, SURROUNDED BY OUR FAMILIES...
THAT'S WHAT I WANT TO PROTECT ...!
... THAT SORT OF SCENE ...
I ALMOST LOST...
...THOSE MEMORIES...
FATHER, MOTHER.
BIG SIS, MY LITTLE BROTHERS.
EVERY-ONE.
MY PRECIOUS FAMILY...
...REALLY? AGAIN?

STILL WORKING ON THIS POND OF YOURS?
...YOU CAUGHT ME.
GYAHHH!
GYAHHH!
...IT'S ABOUT TIME FOR THE SUMMER FESTIVALS BACK IN JAPAN, NOW.
I THOUGHT I MIGHT LET THE KIDS TRY GOLDFISH-SCOOPING...
...YOU GET IT NEXT, HOTARU!
I'M THE BIG SISTER, SO I GO FIRST.
GYAHHH!
GYAHHH!
WHY'S IT MATTER YOU'RE OLDER?
ヒョイ
HYOI (PLUCK)
AH!?

HEYYY!
MINE NOW!
GET BACK HERE!
...
THERE'S ENOUGH FOR EVERYONE.
SO STOP IGHTING!
!
HERE.
PASHA (SPLASH)
LOOK, MOMMY.
I GOT ONE.
I'M GONNA RUN A FISH SHOP WHEN I GROW UP!
YOU'RE GOOD ENOUGH ALREADY!

HOTARU, YOU CAN BE...

...ANYTHING YOU WANT TO BE.

PEOPLE I NEVER WANT TO FORGET.

MEMORIES I NEVER WANT TO LOSE.
THAT'S WHAT I TREASURE ...

...AND THAT'S WHAT SHE WANTS TO PROTECT...

......

ROSE-SAN, THESE GUYS ARE ORPHANS, ACTUALLY.
AH...
IT'S FINE.

...EVEN STREET KIDS LIKE US...
...ONCE HAD FAMILY.

'COS IT'S EASIER T'KEEP IT ALL LOCKED UP INSIDE...
...'N' NOT LET OURSELVES REMEMBER.
...BUT WE NEVER COMPLETELY FORGET.
WE TREASURE THOSE MEMORIES.

...ARE YOU OKAY, ZEL?
YES...

I'M SORRY...
...I'M A MESS.

I'M SORRY IF I UPSET YOU...
KOTO (CLUNK)

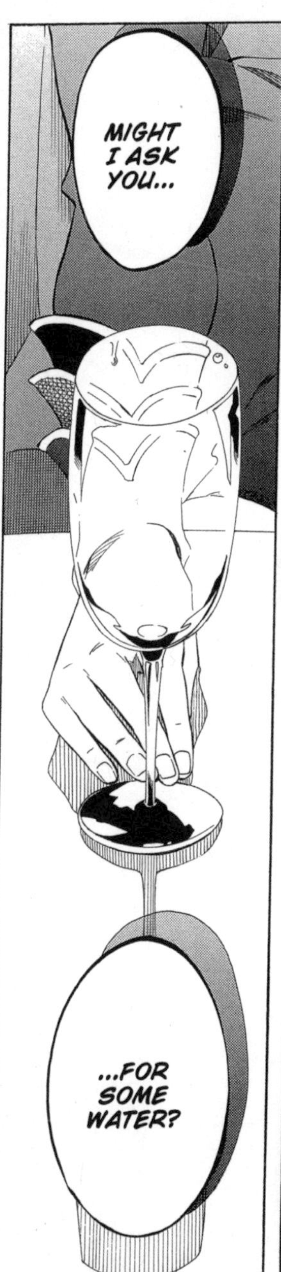
MIGHT I ASK YOU...
...FOR SOME WATER?

I WOULD APPRECIATE IT. SPEAKING SO MUCH HAS MADE MY VOICE RASPY...

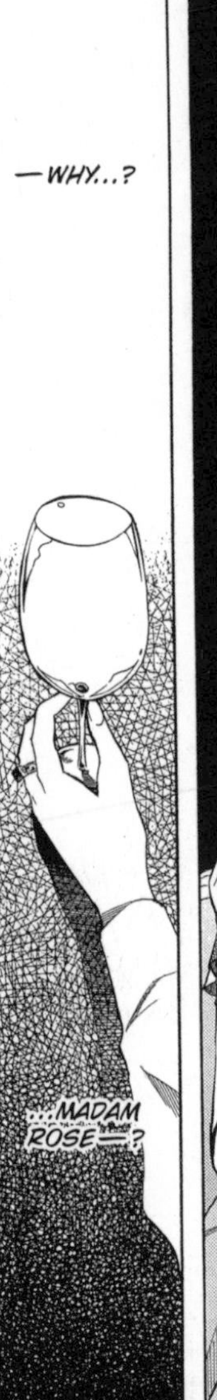
—WHY...?
...MADAM ROSE—?

WHY WOULD YOU TRUST A STRANGER WITHOUT HESITATION?
FURA (WOBBLE)
YOU WERE JUST TALKING ABOUT HOW FOOLISH THE JAPANESE ARE.

SO WHY TRUST ME...?

DOPO (BLUB)
POP
TO SAVE MY FATHER ...
...I HAVE TO KILL HER.
GOTO (CLUNK)
I HAVE TO KILL MADAM ROSE, WHO'S TRYING SO HARD TO PROTECT THOSE MEMORIES FOR EVERYONE...
THEN—
I CAN'T ABANDON EITHER OF THEM.
PACHIN (CLICK)
I CAN'T PRO-TECT BOTH, CAN I?
MORE THAN MEMORIES, I HAVE TO SAVE MY FATHER, WHO'S STILL ALIVE...

I DON'T HAVE A CHOICE ...
THIS IS FOR FATHER...
...TO PROTECT HIM.
I HAVE TO KILL...
—YOU...

... FOOLISH GIRL!

...!

I'M JUST...
—NO.

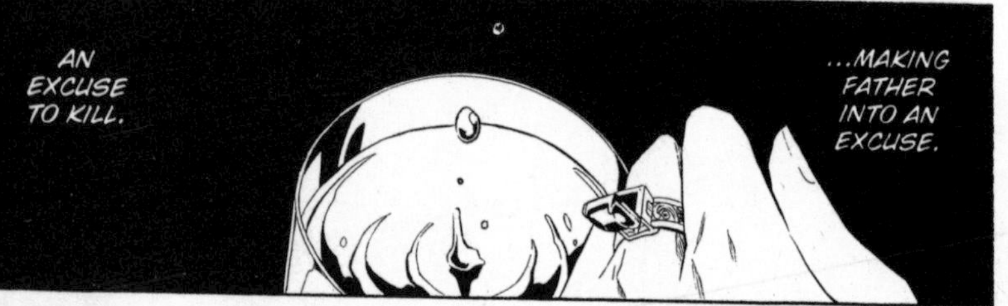
...MAKING FATHER INTO AN EXCUSE.
AN EXCUSE TO KILL.

...I CAN'T DO THAT!
...!

I JUST CAN'T...!
PACHIN (CLICK)

...THANK YOU, ZEL.
FOR GUARDING MY LIFE.
!?
GATA (SPIN)
EH...
...
... WELL, THAT RING...
...DOESN'T SUIT YOU AT ALL...

GASHAN (CLATTER)
ZEL!?
HE'LL BE KILLED...
FATHER...THEY'LL KILL HIM!

JUST LI WHEN LITTLE BROTHE WERE KILLED
LIKE WHEN MOTHER WAS KILLED ...!!
LIKE WHEN BIG SIS WAS KILLED.
NO, DON'T!!
BASHA (SPLASH)

I DON'T WANNA REMEMBER.

DON'T MAKE ME REMEMBER !!!

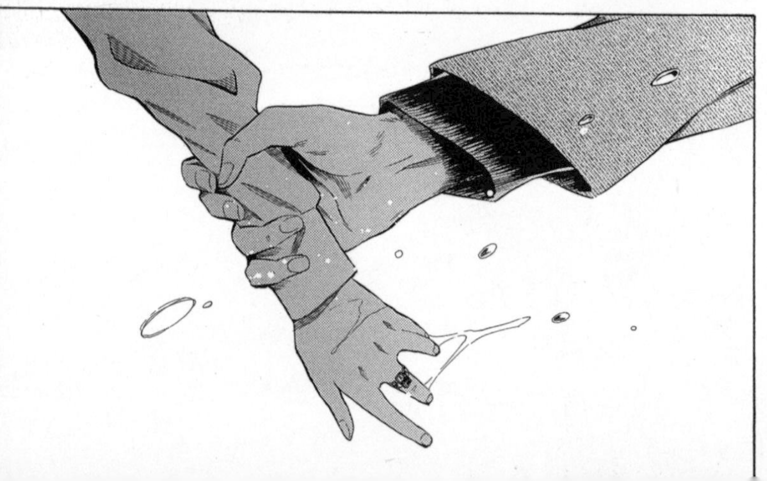

GET OFF ME...

ZEL!

BASHA (SPLASH)

CALM DOWN, ZEL...!

GET OFF MEEEEE!!

WHAT'S WRONG!?

ZEL...
WHAT'S THE BIG IDEA...?
WHAT HAPPENED BACK THERE!?
BASA (FLAP)

...BRING HER BACK TO THE MUSIC SHOP.

MAKE SURE SHE DOESN'T RUN AWAY.

WAYNE-SAN...!?

SOMEONE HIRED HER TO ASSASSINATE MADAM ROSE.

SHE'S A SPY FROM CHINATOWN.

HER CODENAME IS...

...“HOTARUBI.”

...

YOU'RE GONNA TELL US EVERY-THING.
...HOTA-RUBI.

FATHER...

ROSE GUNS DAYS Season 2 2 END

TRANSLATION NOTES

COMMON HONORIFICS

no honorific: Indicates familiarity or closeness; if used without permission or reason, addressing someone in this manner would constitute an insult.

-san: The Japanese equivalent of Mr./Mrs./Miss. If a situation calls for politeness, this is the fail-safe honorific.

-sama: Conveys great respect; may also indicate that the social status of the speaker is lower than that of the addressee.

-kun: Used most often when referring to boys, this indicates affection or familiarity. Occasionally used by older men among their peers, but it may also be used by anyone referring to a person of lower standing.

-chan: An affectionate honorific indicating familiarity used mostly in reference to girls; also used in reference to cute persons or animals of either gender.

-senpai: A suffix used to address upperclassmen or more experienced coworkers.

PAGE 155

Rose is listing some of the most notable **Japanese cultural celebrations** that occur each year, each of which comes with particular customs. For example, Hina Matsuri (also called Girls' Day) revolves around special dolls, while Tanabata is celebrated with large, decorated paper streamers.

PAGE 157

Summer festivals in Japan often involve streets lined with stalls offering food, knick-knacks, and games. One of the most iconic games is "goldfish scooping," in which the player attempts to use a flimsy paper paddle (one that rips easily in water) to flick a live goldfish into a bucket. Zel's father is attempting to recreate that tradition for his family.

ROSE GUNS DAYS
Season2

MUSIC SHOP DAYS 2

THIS WON'T DO, OLIVER.
YOU KNOW THEY SAY THE BEST MEDICINE IS ALWAYS BITTER.
COME ON.
101.3°
SHUT UP, ALREADY!!

IF YOU MAKE ME TAKE THAT NASTY STUFF, I'LL BE IN AN EVEN WORSE MOOD...
I HATE MEDICINE!!
WHEEZE...
HAA...

しゅん…
SHUN (WILT)
BUT... I JUST...

I JUST WANT YOU TO GET BETTER...
GUSU (SNIFFLE)
...!

GA (GULP)
OLIVER'S ACTUALLY TAKING MEDICINE!?
IT'S GOTTA BE A BLUE MOON TONIGHT!!
THE NEXT MORN-ING
SHUT UP!!

CHINESE MEDICINE SURE IS SOMETHING!!
スッキリ
SUKKIRI (REFRESHED)

NO WONDER. THEY'VE HAD 4,000 YEARS TO PERFECT THE ART...
HM,
97.7º...

KOTSUN (PRESS)

A SLIGHT FEVER.

...!!?

BON (PUFF)
104.4º
TOO CLOSE.
JUST LEAVE ME ALONE!!

END

MMM. MMM.

SPECIAL THANKS

NONOSHITA-SAMA

I APPRECIATE YOUR HELP EVERY TIME.

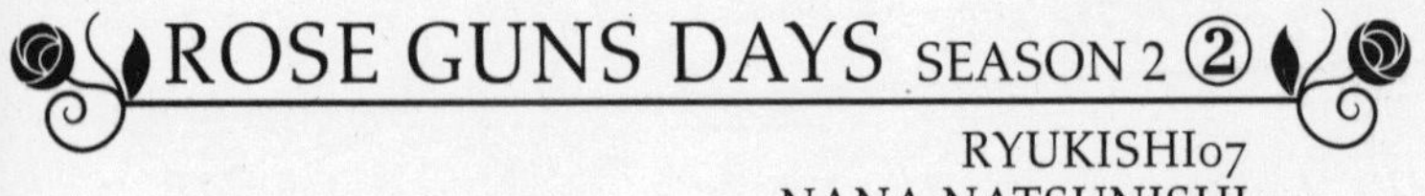

ROSE GUNS DAYS SEASON 2 ②

RYUKISHI07
NANA NATSUNISHI

Translation: Caleb D. Cook • Lettering: Katie Blakeslee and Lys Blakeslee

Yen Press
1290 Avenue of the Americas
New York, NY 10104

Visit us at yenpress.com
facebook.com/yenpress
twitter.com/yenpress
yenpress.tumblr.com
instagram.com/yenpress

First Yen Press Edition: February 2017

Yen Press is an imprint of Yen Press, LLC.
The Yen Press name and logo are trademarks of Yen Press, LLC.

Th ... ed